T0271166

Utilities and Industrial History

This shortform book presents key peer-reviewed research selected by expert series editors and contextualised by new analysis on the industrial history of delivering utilities.

With contributions on the strengths and weaknesses of the creation of electricity networks, the organisation and performance of Britain's nationalised gas industry, and the environmental impact of delivering water and removing waste water, this volume provides an array of fascinating insights into industrial history.

Of interest to business and economic historians, this shortform book also provides analysis and illustrative case-studies that will be valuable reading across the social sciences.

John F. Wilson is the Pro Vice-Chancellor (Business and Law) at Northumbria University, Newcastle. He has published widely in the fields of business, management, and industrial history, including ten monographs, six edited collections, and over seventy articles and chapters.

Steven Toms is a Professor of Accounting at the University of Leeds. He is a former editor of Business History. His research interests are focused on accounting and financial history and the history of the textile industry.

Ian G. Jones is a Senior Research Assistant at Newcastle Business School, Northumbria University, winner of the 2022 Coleman Prize for best PhD thesis in business history, and won the John F. Mee Best Paper Award at the Academy of Management in 2018 for his contribution to the Management History Division.

Routledge Focus on Industrial History
Series Editors: John F. Wilson, Steven Toms and Ian G. Jones

This shortform series presents key peer-reviewed research originally published in the *Journal of Industrial History*, selected by expert series editors and contextualised by new analysis from each author on how the specific field addressed has evolved.

Of interest to business historians, economic historians and social scientists interested in the development of key industries, the series makes theoretical and conceptual contributions to the field, as well as providing a plethora of empirical, illustrative and detailed case studies of industrial developments in Britain, the United States and other international settings.

Knowledge Management
Dependency, Creation and Loss in Industrial History
Edited by John F. Wilson, Ian G. Jones and Steven Toms

The Development of Professional Management
Training, Consultancy, and Management Theory in Industrial History
Edited by John F. Wilson, Ian G. Jones and Steven Toms

Forms of Organising in Industrial History
Edited by John F. Wilson, Steven Toms and Ian G. Jones

Utilities and Industrial History
Edited by John F. Wilson, Steven Toms and Ian G. Jones

For more information about this series, please visit: www.routledge.com/Routledge-Focus-on-Industrial-History/book-series/RFIH

Utilities and Industrial History

**Edited by
John F. Wilson, Steven Toms and
Ian G. Jones**

Routledge
Taylor & Francis Group

LONDON AND NEW YORK

First published 2023
by Routledge
4 Park Square, Milton Park, Abingdon, Oxon OX14 4RN

and by Routledge
605 Third Avenue, New York, NY 10158

Routledge is an imprint of the Taylor & Francis Group, an informa business

© 2023 selection and editorial matter, John F. Wilson, Steven Toms
and Ian G. Jones; individual chapters, the contributors

The right of John F. Wilson, Steven Toms and Ian G. Jones to be
identified as the authors of the editorial material, and of the authors
for their individual chapters, has been asserted in accordance with
sections 77 and 78 of the Copyright, Designs and Patents Act 1988.

All rights reserved. No part of this book may be reprinted or
reproduced or utilised in any form or by any electronic, mechanical,
or other means, now known or hereafter invented, including
photocopying and recording, or in any information storage or
retrieval system, without permission in writing from the publishers.

Trademark notice: Product or corporate names may be trademarks
or registered trademarks, and are used only for identification and
explanation without intent to infringe.

British Library Cataloguing-in-Publication Data
A catalogue record for this book is available from the British Library

Library of Congress Cataloging-in-Publication Data
Names: Wilson, John F. (Vice-Chancellor), editor.
Title: Utilities and industrial history / edited by John F. Wilson,
Steven Toms and Ian G. Jones.
Description: Abingdon, Oxon ; New York, NY : Routledge, [2023] |
Series: Routledge focus on industrial history | Includes
bibliographical references and index.
Identifiers: LCCN 2022020826 (print) | LCCN 2022020827 (ebook) |
ISBN 9781032363509 (hbk) | ISBN 9781032363516 (pbk) |
ISBN 9781003331506 (ebk)
Subjects: LCSH: Electric utilities—Great Britain. | Gas industry—
Great Britain. | Water—Pollution—Great Britain.
Classification: LCC HD2765.G72 U85 2023 (print) |
LCC HD2765.G72 (ebook) | DDC 363.60973—dc23/eng/20220711
LC record available at https://lccn.loc.gov/2022020826
LC ebook record available at https://lccn.loc.gov/2022020827

ISBN: 978-1-032-36350-9 (hbk)
ISBN: 978-1-032-36351-6 (pbk)
ISBN: 978-1-003-33150-6 (ebk)

DOI: 10.4324/9781003331506

Typeset in Times New Roman
by codeMantra

Contents

Contents

Figures

Tables

Contributors

John Hassan was a Senior Lecturer at Manchester Metropolitan University and published the book *A History of Water* (Manchester University Press).

Andrew Jenkins is an Associate Professor in the Social Research Institute at University College London. Andrew's research focuses on adult learning, higher education, and the application of quantitative methods in educational research, with his research being published in a variety of journals, including *British Journal of Educational Studies, Business History*, and *Applied Economics*. Andrew has also written several books, including *Bread and the British Economy, 1770–1870* (Routledge) with Christian Petersen, as well as contributing to *Improving Literacy at Work* (Routledge).

Alan Jones completed his PhD thesis at the University of Wales with his thesis titled The Introduction and Development of Electricity in the South Wales Coal Industry up to 1926.

1 Introduction

John F. Wilson, Ian G. Jones and Steven Toms

1 Purpose and significance of the series

The concept of the *Routledge Focus on Industrial History* series was motivated by the desire of the editors to provide an outlet for articles originally published in the defunct *Journal of Industrial History (JIH)*. By using an extensive repository of top-quality publications, the series will ensure that the authors' findings contribute to recent debates in the field of management and industrial history. Indeed, the articles contained in these volumes will appeal to a wide audience, including business historians, economic historians, and social scientists interested in longitudinal studies of the development of key industries and themes. Moreover, the series will provide fresh insight into how the academic field has developed over the past 20 years.

The editors believe that the quality of scholarship evident in the articles originally published in the *JIH* now deserves a much broader audience. The peer-reviewed articles are built on robust business-historical research methodologies and are subject to extensive primary research. The series will make important theoretical and conceptual contributions to the field and provide a plethora of empirical, illustrative, and detailed case studies of industrial developments in the United Kingdom, the United States, and other international settings. The collection will be of interest to a broad stratum of social scientists, especially business school and history department academics, because it provides valuable material that can be used in both teaching and research.

2 Building on the original *Journal of Industrial History*

The first edition of the *Journal of Industrial History* was published in 1998, with the aim of providing 'clear definitional parameters for industrial historians' and, in turn, establishing links between

DOI: 10.4324/9781003331506-1

'industrial history and theoretical work in social science disciplines like economics, management (including international business), political science, sociology, and anthropology'. Because it has been more than 20 years since its original publication, it is clear that the relevance of the *JIH* has stood the test of time. The original *JIH* volumes covered a diverse range of topics, including industrial structure and behaviour, especially in manufacturing and services; industrial and business case studies; business strategy and structure; nationalisation and privatisation; globalisation and competitive advantage; business culture and industrial development; education, training, and human resources; industrial relations and its institutions; the relationship between financial institutions and industry; industrial politics, including the formulation and impact of industrial and commercial policy; and industry and technology. The current *Routledge Focus on Industrial History* series will provide a cross-section of articles that cover a wide range of themes and topics, many of which remain central to management studies. These include separate volumes: *Knowledge Management: Dependency, Creation, and Loss in Industrial History, A Search for Competitive Advantage in Industrial History*, and *The Role of Government in Markets: Interventions and Unexpected Consequences in Industrial History*. The *Routledge Focus on Industrial History* series will reframe highly original material that illustrates a wide variety of themes in management and organisation studies, including entrepreneurship, strategy, family business, trust, networks, and international business, focusing on topics such as the growth of the firm, crisis management, governance, management, and leadership.

3 Volume Eleven

The first chapter, 'The role of the consulting engineer in the electrification of the South Wales coal industry up to about 1926' by Alan Jones, discusses the development of various electricity grids at collieries and Local Authority public lighting networks in South Wales. This chapter focuses on the role of consultants in the process of designing, constructing, and maintaining these systems, arguing that part of the reason that the design of these systems was so eclectic – an issue that would create future problems when they needed to be expanded or linked to other networks – was due to the lack of skilled engineers and the high demand for their continuing services in maintaining the systems. However, the chapter also shows that whilst these engineers may have preferred to use designs they were already familiar with rather than working towards standardisation, the designs requested by collieries and Local Authorities favoured the cheapest solutions over those that could be expanded to meet future demand, further stymieing movement towards standardisation. Despite these problems, successful systems were implemented in collieries, stimulating demand from others, and creating demand for consulting engineers' skills. Therefore, scarcity of knowledge in the form of qualified engineers and the demands for cheap systems from customers that harmed standardisation efforts appear to also have been responsible for the later problems encountered when expanding and integrating electricity networks.

The second chapter, 'The British gas industry, 1949 to 1970: a regional comparison' by Andrew Jenkins, focuses on the performance of two nationalised regional gas boards – the South Western (SWGB) and the East Midlands (EMGB) – and examines the main factors that influenced their long-term strategies. This chapter shows that, despite being nationalised industries, the regional context in which they operated cannot be overlooked when assessing their performance and in understanding the production and marketing strategies they pursued. Before the discovery and exploitation of North Sea gas, which required centralised plans to develop and distribute it, Area Gas Boards were more powerful than in other nationalised industries, setting their own tariffs, producing their own production plans, and being financially autonomous. There were also regional differences in the demand for gas and how it could be produced, with the EMGB having far more industrial customers and a greater number of methods for producing gas than the SWGB. These difficulties led to poorer economic performance from the SWGB than the EMGB, leading to a greater focus on cost cutting and efficiencies which also affected their marketing and advertising strategies, with EMGB able to dedicate more resources to marketing towards new customers and engaging in market research. Despite being nationalised industries that ostensibly supplied the same products, regional and local contexts as well the decisions of Area Gas Boards have to be taken into account to fully understand how the gas industry operated during this time.

The third chapter, 'Industrialisation, pollution and estuarine rescue' by John Hassan, highlights the environmental impact of industry through waste disposal, in particular, the effects of waste disposal on water pollution in the Mersey and the Tyne Rivers. Hassan shows the necessity of taking a historical approach to understand this issue, as many of the pollutants created by industry had negligible effects in the short term; only once they had built up beyond the natural environment's ability to dilute and purify them did the impact become apparent, something which could take decades. However, Hassan makes clear that it is not just industrial waste that can be a problem, conceiving of water and waste water as joint products as the consumption of water by households, businesses, or industry inevitably results in waste water. Conceiving of water this way forms part of Hassan's four-stage model, which demonstrates firstly how water and waste water are intimately connected; secondly, the period of time it took before the assimilative capacity of local water ways were overwhelmed and how this affected the local human and animal populations; thirdly, the conflicts of interest that prevented remedial action being taken earlier; and fourthly, the confluence of interests that lead to active efforts at estuarine rescue. This chapter remains relevant to discussions on the environmental impact of society today, highlighting the environmental impact of the consumption of basic resources, such as water, and the need to take a long-term view when assessing the environmental impact of human behaviour.

4 Conclusion

It is apparent from this brief review of the chapter that the eleventh volume in the series makes important contributions to the field of industrial history in several ways. Firstly, it provides a series of high-calibre and unique studies in aspects of industrial history that contribute to more recent debates on the environmental impact of human behaviour, the performance of nationalised industry vs. private industry, and how both producers and consumers affect standardisation of a product. Secondly, the chapters shed light on the broader subjects of knowledge management, environmental protection, and energy production and scarcity. Finally, this volume provides strong historical case studies that can be used by students and researchers who are exploring issues related to the delivery of utilities in the United Kingdom. The editors believe that this volume will not only provide a much wider audience for articles that link into a range of topical issues but also feed into debates in the wider social sciences. These are themes that were demonstrated in previous volumes in the *Routledge Series of Industrial History*, highlighting the intrinsic value in republishing material from the *Journal of Industrial History* and ensuring that the articles contribute extensively to current debates.

2 The role of the consulting engineer in the electrification of the South Wales coal industry up to about 1926[*]

Alan Jones

1 Introduction

In theory the role of the consulting engineer is an invaluable one. Unlike commercial interests, who are mainly concerned with increasing the sales of their own products, consulting engineers are able to take an independent and broader view of the industry and hence act in the best interest of their clients. However, considering the perceived importance of his role, the consulting engineer has received relatively little attention from economic historians or those studying the history of engineering and technology. What attention he has received has been largely concerned with his role and effectiveness during the early years of the British electrical supply industry (ESI). Much of the comment has been negative in respect that individual preference, self promotion and the consulting engineers' widespread practice of accepting the lowest tender actually retarded the standardisation of electrical products at a critical stage in Britain's electrical development. The lack of standardisation has, in turn, been claimed to have placed the early British electrical equipment manufacturers at a competitive disadvantage with their American and Continental counterparts, increased the first cost of the equipment, decreased reliability and the quality of the finished product.

This paper, therefore, attempts to answer the question: was the level of criticism directed at the consulting engineer in the early days of the ESI representative of his prowess in other industrial sectors? The answer to this question will not be considered in a general industrial context, but rather in one specific sector – that of the coal industry and, in particular, within south Wales, a major coal producing region and one which was particularly innovative and progressive in the early use of electricity

After outlining the function of the consulting engineer in section 2, section 3 outlines ongoing controversy of the role of the consulting

DOI: 10.4324/9781003331506-2

engineer, particularly in British industry between about 1875 and 1914. Section 4 then considers the early years of the ESI and Section 5 focuses on the role of the consulting engineer and his general contribution towards the electrification of the South Wales coal industry, as well as identifying specific colliery installations. The conclusions reached are that a number of positive aspects were realised through the use of consulting engineers within the south Wales coal industry when compared with his counterpart in the ESI. The most positive aspect may have arisen out of circumstance, since the initiative to establish electricity within the South Wales coal industry was initially very much the prerogative of a small number of medium-to-large colliery companies, who were able to raise the high capital expenditure required for schemes, many of which were substantial and included self-generation. In an attempt to minimise risks and safeguard such an investment, these colliery owners drew upon the services of a very small number of consulting engineers having proven experience and specialist knowledge. This limiting of expertise to a handful of high-profile engineers prevented a proliferation of designs that meant that many standard and proven features could be implemented. A number of these electrification schemes quickly became 'model' systems and received wide publicity and, as such, provided the stimulus for other concerns to implement electricity, or to engage the very same engineers themselves. This meant that many of the early colliery electrification schemes in South Wales possessed a high degree of compatibility, efficiency and reliability, something which was not achieved by consulting engineers engaged in the ESI.

2 The function of the consulting electrical engineer

In the early 1890s, a consulting electrical engineer advising a Local Authority (LA) considering the installation of an electricity generating station would, after site visits and establishing his clients exact requirements, produce a report indicating the feasibility, or otherwise, of such a venture.[1] The report, which was produced on the basis of a previously agreed fixed fee, usually in the form of a one-off payment, would typically include: the options as to the 'best' electrical system, i.e. a.c. or d.c (high- or low-tension); the make, type, rating (in kW or h.p.) and cost of generating equipment, prime-mover, ancillary equipment, switchgear and cabling; estimates for the construction of the power house, offices, out-buildings, etc.; estimate for excavation work, e.g. the digging up (and making good) of streets to lay underground cables; estimates of revenue and maintenance (including the identification and cost of specialist labour, e.g. linesmen, superintendents; advice on the obtaining of Provisional Orders (POs) or Licences, and relevant plans and sketches. If the LA decided to accept the consulting engineer's proposals, additional fees would then have to be negotiated if assistance in obtaining POs or Licences, or the placing of orders and contracts was required.

The acceptance of lowest price tenders was not initially established practice for electrical plant. By 1895 the situation had changed, with consulting engineers becoming more independent of the manufacturers. This 'distancing' meant that specifications were more detailed, responsibility for the design lay now with the consulting engineer and the awarding of contracts concentrated on the lowest tender price.[2] Therefore, prior to this date it is not possible to know whether the estimates submitted by the early consulting engineers to their clients were in fact the lowest prices or whether they included an element of mark-up for the consulting engineer himself.

When the acceptance of best or lowest price tenders became a widely established practice, evidence exists to show that in at least one colliery company the consulting engineer was subject to a vetting procedure. In 1907 when the directors of the Locket's Merthyr Colliery Company Limited instructed their consulting engineer to obtain prices for the supply and erection of generating plant at their Mardy colliery in south Wales, they requested that he submit to them a list of the six or seven lowest or best price tenders.[3] However, more than a suspicion exists that the acceptance of lowest price tender was sometimes waived when the consulting engineer could show to his clients that one particular make of equipment had a distinct technical advantage over another, or had a record of proven in-service reliability.[4]

By the late 1920s the role of the consulting engineer in the coal industry, with perhaps with a few exceptions, was still essentially that of him being paid for a specific task or retained on an annual fee and providing technical advice and guidance as and when required. The major exception was that the consulting engineer was now much more accountable to his client, in that it was now fairly standard practice for him to channel all paperwork and correspondence, including estimates, through the colliery office (usually through the General Manager), as opposed to just presenting the final recommendations to his client. Also, a greater onus was placed upon equipment integrity, because the consulting engineer himself was now normally expected to test and inspect equipment prior to it leaving the manufacturers premises, and once installed he was required to carry out periodic testing and inspection of the plant and report upon its condition.[5]

It would appear that the 'rule of thumb' as to whether a colliery company should employ a permanent electrical engineer or call upon a consulting engineer, depended upon the maximum daily output of coal. If this figure was below 1000 tons/day then it was considered more economical to engage a consulting engineer.[6]

3   The consulting engineer controversy

Recent commentators have been generally critical of the early development of British industry in two main areas, namely, its slow development when compared to America and the Continent, and the lack of standardisation of product design which also inhibited rapid growth and development.

Saul, who has written widely on the development of British industry and foreign competition, has identified a number of reasons as to why British industry from about 1870 onwards declined at the cost of the Americans and the Germans. One of the weaknesses, he contended, writing in 1960, was that of the use of the consulting engineer, who '... ignored commercial factors because he had no stake in the matter beyond his fee'.[7] Then, in 1968, Saul further criticised the consulting engineer, who, whilst present throughout all branches of industry predominated in the civil, locomotive and, later, electrical sectors, tended to '... design a product of high technical quality which would do him credit in his profession'.[8] Such an approach meant that his clients were not always able to obtain products at the lowest cost and, perhaps more importantly, these one-off designs prevented the standardisation of product that was so necessary if economies of scale and more effective marketing were to be realised by the manufacturer.

In the same year (1968) Aldcroft also acknowledged that there were a number of factors which contributed to the comparative backwardness of certain sectors of British industry, one of which was the dominance of the consulting engineer (particularly in electrical engineering) who 'tended to inhibit product standardisation and limit the market power of individual firms'.[9]

Byatt, writing in 1977, was also of the opinion that the slow rate of innovation of electrical plant design in Britain's electrical industry was because of competitive tendering, with the consulting engineer playing a crucial role.[10] Such a practice, he stated, was in marked contrast to that in America or on the Continent, where electrical equipment manufacturers retained much more influence and were able to offer 'standard' designs incorporating many proven features. Hannah, on the other hand, in 1979, believed that the 'rich variety' of voltages and frequencies adopted by British electricity supply undertakings was difficult to explain in terms other than the 'individualism of British engineers', and that the strength of municipal suppliers and the absence of close links between them and the equipment manufacturers only served to further exacerbate the problem.[11]

A few years later, in 1983, Hughes supported Hannah's views that the state of Britain's electricity supply prior to the First World War, in that it was 'towards variation, not standardisation'.[12] Hughes believed that such a situation had arisen through the absence of 'oligopoly in the electrical manufacturing industry and the prestige and influence of the consulting engineer'. In 1988 Wilson expressed similar sentiments to Byatt, arguing that the sluggish development of the British electrical industry in the 1880s put the home market at a disadvantage when compared to their German and American counterparts. This problem, he believed, was further exacerbated by a slump in the early 1890s and by '... various structural weaknesses in the British market', in particular the use of consulting engineers who prevented standardisation and introduced onerous contractual obligations.[13] Then, in 1995, Wilson referred to the 'ubiquitous feature' of the consulting engineer in British engineering, drawing attention to the fact that in electrical engineering, in particular, his insistence on producing detailed specifications '... prevented the standardisation of product which was so rapidly developing in the USA'.[14]

Contemporaries were also aware of the problems of Britain's ESI and the practices of the consulting engineer. Sellon, in a widely publicised paper in 1900, stressed the need for standardised electrical equipment, and indicated the advantages that standardisation gave to both manufacturer and customer.[15] For the customer it offered lower capital costs, improved equipment reliability and a greater likelihood of meeting contractual obligations. Sellon firmly believed that standardisation would enable British electrical plant manufacturers to compete more effectively against their American and Continental counterparts, for whom standard or repetitive manufacture was very much an established practice.

In Sellon's mind consulting engineers were primarily responsible for the relative absence of standardisation of electrical plant in Britain, because firstly they insisted upon detailing the workings of the equipment as opposed to stating the 'end use', and leaving the manufacturers to undertake the detailed design. Secondly, there was the ability of the consulting engineer himself – he might be 'out of touch', having limited experience or, even, incompetent. Thirdly, he simply wanted to impress his clients with novelty and/or unnecessary features (and, hence, enhance his own reputation and be retained or considered for future contracts); and, finally, the widespread practice of accepting lowest tender, which was a condition imposed upon him by his clients. As we have already indicated, the problem with the acceptance of lowest price tender was that it could result in poor quality and unreliable equipment as manufacturers sought to secure contracts in a highly competitive market.

Sellon identified local authorities (LAs), who relied heavily upon the use of consulting engineers, as the main culprits in encouraging the proliferation of non-standard designs (see Table 2.1), through insisting upon the acceptance of the lowest price tender, as an ever increasing number began installing local, electricity supply systems, primarily for lighting purposes.

In 1901, when giving evidence before the Institution of Electrical Engineers Committee on Electrical Legislation, Lt-Col R. E.

Table 2.1 Summary of analysis of the divergence of technical choice amongst electricity supply systems installed by British LAs in 1900

a) Number of generating stations and type of system

D.C. (three-wire) systems	D.C. (HT) Systems	A.C. Systems	Generating both A.C. and D.C. systems
73	9	62	16

Key: D.C. – direct current, HT – high tension, A.C. – alternating current

b) Number of generating stations producing a supply at a frequency of:

A	100	98	90	87	83	80	77	75	70	67	60	50	40
B	20	2	2	2	7	4	1	3	1	2	8	20	3

Key: A – frequency of supply (Hz), B – number of generating stations

c) Number of generating stations producing an a.c. supply at various voltages
Number of generating stations producing an a.c. supply at a voltage of:

C	10,000	8,000	2,600–2,400	2,200–2,000	1,800–1,600	1,000
D	1	2	2	66	1	1

Key: C – supply voltage (Va.c.), D – number of generating stations

Note: Although there are minor errors in Sellon's figures, they well illustrate the diversity of technical choice that existed amongst Britain's LAs as early as 1900.

Crompton, a leading British designer, consultant and manufacturer of all kinds of electrical machinery since 1878, was deeply critical of the way in which British electrical manufacturers had failed to advance at the same rate as Germany, Switzerland and elsewhere, despite leading at one time.[16] Whilst he attributed some of this backwardness to that of restrictive legislation (which strongly favoured parochial interests) arising from the 1882 and 1888 Electric Lighting Acts, he was strongly of the opinion that the main cause was that of individual requirements, not just from the consulting engineers themselves but also by the engineers permanently employed by the Statutory Undertakings.[17]

Another contemporary opinion as to the problems arising from the acceptance of lowest tender, and the role of the consulting and/or resident engineers in the ESI was made by C. P. Sparks, twice President of the Institution of Electrical Engineers and a prominent consulting engineer himself, on two different occasions in 1915:

> ... the onus of development and the successful carrying out of a contract are borne by the contractor, and if a reasonable margin of profit is not secured, the contractor cannot in the long run do his duty by the purchasers. First, the contractor is crippled, being unable to make provision for development, since without profit new capital cannot be attracted; but what is more serious, provisions cannot be made for improvements, without which we cannot keep pace with our world competitors.
>
> It is not that engineers do not recognise what is the right principle: it is the human factor. In many districts if a supply is offered in bulk it does not matter how low a price is mentioned, the local engineer at once draws up a scheme showing that he can provide the supply for less. He convinces the committee and he retains his job.[18]

Although it was evident by the beginning of the twentieth century that Britain's ESI was largely organised around the consulting engineer, this had not always been the case. In fact, the practice of consulting engineers, particularly on planned regional electrification by LAs, did not become widely established prior to about 1895, as the next section shows.

4 The early years of the electrical supply industry

In the mid 1870s electricity finally became a practical reality through the introduction of the d.c. generator by Z. T. Gramme, since his machine produced a steady output voltage and could run for long periods without overheating. Initially D.C. generators were used to supply lighting schemes (arc and, later, incandescent lighting), but within a decade power applications were becoming increasingly common. The design, procurement, installation and commissioning of such schemes initially lay very much in the hands of a relatively small number of electrical manufacturers or their appointed agents – essentially those who possessed the necessary technical knowledge, expertise and, perhaps more importantly, on-going support in the case of breakdown. As the demand for electric lighting increased, a number of electricians who were previously employed or linked to these electrical manufacturers set themselves up in their own right. An early prominent figure in Britain was that of S. F. Walker who, after working as an engineer for the Gramme Magneto Engineering Company, set himself up as an independent 'pioneer contractor' with offices in Nottingham, Leeds, Sheffield and Cardiff.[19] Walker installed some of the first Gramme dynamos in Britain and by the early 1880s much of his time was spent installing electric lighting schemes in coal mines, especially in south Wales.[20] Such was his success that within a few years he had become Britain's foremost authority on colliery electric lighting. Exactly how 'independent' Walker was is uncertain, but given his background and that available evidence indicates that he exclusively installed Gramme machines suggests a close working relationship and, possibly, some kind of preferential supply agreement with the equipment manufacturers. Whatever the case, his practice was clearly not based on cost considerations alone, since a typical Gramme machine had a considerably higher first cost than its Siemens equivalent, i.e. £320 compared to £265 (1873 figures).[21] Since the efficiency and the reliability of these machines are not known, it is not possible to say whether these were factors in opting for the more expensive machine.

Although Walker was an early, successful consulting engineer who preferred to describe himself as a 'pioneer contractor', he, and others who followed, were not able to make any major impact upon the embryonic British market, but rather found niche applications. The main ESI market was left to the large electrical manufacturers which included such British companies as Crompton and Ferranti, and, more particularly, overseas companies which included Brush, Edison, Siemens, Thompson, Westinghouse and General Electric (of America): many of the latter having British subsidiaries and employing their own design, installation and commissioning engineers. Occasionally, such companies, for example the American General Electric, later had their engineers undertaking research on electrical problems generally, and acting on a consultancy basis.[22]

Although a relatively large number of companies vied for a small, albeit growing market, the practice of selecting through competitive tender was not initially the norm. This practice, as we have previously indicated, only began to establish itself in the early to mid 1890s when an increasing number of LAs began to consider electricity as an alternative form of lighting to that of the well-established gas lighting.

The immediate problem facing LAs who contemplated installing electric lighting schemes was the lack of in-house expertise. True, some thought that it was as simple a matter as the resident or local municipal gas engineer or plumber 'changing hats', but the majority rightly acknowledged their lack of existing expertise and sought advice from appropriately qualified electrical engineers. If requested, the Institution of Electrical Engineers provided a list of members who were consultants, but the services of such engineers did not come cheaply, with typical fees (in 1894) for producing a feasibility study being between £10 and 100 guineas.[23] Apart from personal recommendation, the task of selecting a competent engineer by any other method was not an easy matter. Many LAs, in this respect, did not help the situation by applying the same selection criteria to consulting engineers as they used for engaging builders; that is the acceptance of lowest price or tender, and consequently quality and unbiased advice could not always be guaranteed. For at least one LA (Abergavenny, in South Wales) the continued insistence upon engaging consulting engineers on this basis was a major factor in delaying the implementation of public electricity for many decades.[24]

Once appointed by an LA the consulting engineer, although responsible for all the design work, the preparation of drawings and specifications, he was normally obligated to obtain electrical equipment on a lowest cost basis. This, of course, begs the question: just how much were consulting engineers able to represent the best interests of their clients? Certainly the consulting engineer was expected to obtain maximum concessions from potential suppliers, even to the extent of 'playing one off against the other'. However, the major drawback of the lowest cost or 'best price' tenders was to further intensify competition amongst the electrical manufacturers and, hence, equipment quality could suffer as manufacturers sought to secure much needed contracts. Such trading conditions were also likely to reduce the incentive for manufacturers to introduce modifications or improve the performance of their equipment. However, one positive aspect of competitive tendering was that it reduced the dependence of the customer upon one particular manufacturer and provided a means of critical evaluation of different products. With consulting engineers specifying their individual preferences for equipment, non-standard systems proliferated, but one would have thought that this could conflict with lowest price tendering. Whilst this created little problem when electrical systems were self-contained through technical and legislative constraints, it was to introduce major problems when, following the introduction of the 1926 Electricity Supply Act, moves were made to implement an integrated, nation-wide electricity supply system.[25] The diversity of technical choice alone by 1900 was already considerable, as we have already seen from a summary of Sellon's analysis of British electricity supply systems in Table 2.1.

By 1917, Britain's electricity supply system was still very much one of variation, despite the war effort highlighting its weak and fragmentary nature.[26] Probably the best example of such variation was seen in the Greater London area, where it was reported that '... 70 local authorities supply electricity to the public, and own some 70 generating stations, with 50 different types of system, 10 different frequencies and 20 different voltages'.[27]

From the foregoing it is easy to obtain the impression that consulting engineers were very much a negative force in the early years of the British electrical industry through their failure to establish more homogeneous systems, and for this criticism must come their way. However, where consulting engineers, having the ability to look at the wider issues of electricity supply and develop close working relationships with equipment manufacturers were engaged, the outcome was much more successful. Perhaps the outstanding example was C. H. Merz, who master-minded the Newcastle Electric Supply Company (NESCo) such that by 1914 it had emerged from a local undertaking to become a highly integrated network supplying an area of more than 1,400 square miles and providing some of the cheapest electricity in the world.[28] In the private sector, C. P. Sparks was responsible for the master-minding of electrification within the Powell Duffryn Steam Coal Company (hereafter, Powell Duffryn) in South Wales, which in 1915 had a generating capacity of 24,000 kW and an installed motor load of 44,800 h.p.[29]

In addition to Sparks, a number of other high profile consulting engineers were retained by various colliery companies within south Wales to advise on substantial electrification schemes, many of which involved self-generation and onerous working conditions. The next section will consider the introduction and development of electricity in the South Wales coal industry, before leading on to consider the actual role of the consulting engineer and identify specific installations.

5 Electrification in the South Wales coal industry

5.1 Introduction

A recent study by Jones[30] showed that the growth pattern of electrification within the South Wales coal industry was such that by 1914 the region had quickly established itself as the leading user of electricity within the British coal industry – a position which it still maintained in 1926. Whilst Jones's study did not specifically deal with the role of the consulting engineer in this electrification process, it was apparent that the early success and subsequent expansion of a number of colliery electrification schemes (many of which were substantial and involved self-generation) was not only due to the initiative of some colliery owners in an attempt to offset the low profitability normally associated with the coal industry, but also to the ability and vision of a small number of high-calibre consulting engineers. The undoubted success of a number of these consulting engineer-led colliery installations appears to contradict the largely negative role that has been portrayed of the consulting engineer working in the ESI. Therefore, the contribution made by consulting engineers within the South Wales coal industry needs to be considered in greater detail, but first an overview of the growth of electricity in the South Wales coal industry needs to be presented.

5.2 The growth of electricity in the South Wales coal industry: an overview

Table 2.2 shows that by 1905 four colliery companies located in the steam and bituminous coal producing regions of South Wales had installed significant electrical systems (>1,000 kW), some including self-generation. By 1915 the number of colliery companies having installed generating capacities in excess of 1,000 kW had increased to seven, with one company (Powell Duffryn) having an installed generating capacity of 24,000 kW.[31] By 1921 a dozen medium-to-large colliery companies located in the steam coal regions of Glamorgan and the western part of Monmouthshire had installed generating capacities exceeding 1,000 kW.

Table 2.3 shows the total aggregate horsepower installed and the number of mines electrified, together with the figures for installed horsepower per mine, in Britain's coal producing regions. It can be seen that South Wales had, by 1913, established a clear lead, with 181,8181 h.p. (at nearly 29% of the British total); a position which it still maintained in 1926, with 409,744 h.p. (25.3% of the British Isles).

Table 2.2 Installed generating capacity (kW) of various colliery companies
in South Wales, for various years between 1905 and 1921

Year	Number of colliery companies having an installed generating capacity (kW) of:					
	1,000 –4,999	5,000 –9,999	10,000 –14,999	15,000 –19,999	20,000 –24,999	>25,000
1905	4					
1915	6				1	
1921	6	4			1	1

Source: Compiled from Jones, A. V.: The Introduction and Development of Electricity
in the South Wales Coal Industry up to 1926, Ph.D. thesis, Cardiff, 1999.

The evidences of Tables 2.2 and 2.3 suggests that the pattern of
electrification within the British coal industry was very much one of a
relatively small number of medium-to-large colliery companies within
the individual coal-producing regions installing large-scale electrical systems. In South Wales, for example, Powell Duffryn's electrical
system in 1915 accounted for 17% of the coalfield's installed aggregate electrical horsepower.[32] Stretton very effectively summed up the
electrification process that was taking place in South Wales when
he stated that the total generating capacity of plant installed in the
fourteen leading colliery companies (in 1921) stood at 102,140 kW. Of
this 102,140 kW, 65% was installed by four companies, namely, Powell
Duffryn (27,600 kW), Ebbw Vale Iron & Steel Company (22,650 kW),
D. Davis & Sons (8,800 kW) and Tredegar Iron Company (7,350kW).[33]
   All of these companies initially relied heavily upon the services of
consulting engineers and the next section will examine their actual
role in greater detail together, where appropriate, with descriptions of
the actual systems themselves.

5.3 Consulting engineers and specific colliery installations

In Section 4.0 S. F. Walker was identified as one of the earliest consulting engineers specialising in designing and installing electrical lighting systems in collieries. Some of his earliest arc lighting systems (in
1879) were at the Cymmer and Mardy collieries in the then county
of Glamorgan.[34] By 1882 Walker had replaced the arc lights at these
collieries with the recently introduced incandescent lighting, as well as
installing similar schemes in other collieries in Glamorgan and Monmouthshire.[35] In fact Walker was so enthusiastic about the superiority
of electric lighting that, for at least one South Wales colliery company,

he agreed to install a complete electrical system and maintain it for three months at no charge. If, after that time, the colliery owner was not happy with the system, Walker agreed to remove it – again at his own cost. In fact the only financial commitment upon his client over this three-month period was that he had to provide the motive power (steam engine) to the dynamo.[36]

No doubt largely due to Walker's enthusiasm, the success of his early schemes and papers presented before the South Wales Institute of Engineers and elsewhere, interest in electric lighting by South Wales colliery owners was such that by 1889 at least 20 collieries had electric lighting installations (compared to 22 for the rest of Britain).[37] By 1894 the figure for South Wales had risen to 35. Two years later there were only a few collieries in the Rhondda valley without electric lighting and by 1904 electric lighting had been installed in 27 collieries in the county of Monmouthshire.[38]

Although electricity for power purposes had been installed in the nearby Forest of Dean coalfield by 1882, the earliest recorded application of electricity for power purpo'ses in a South Wales colliery was

Table 2.3 Aggregate electrical horsepower installed in Britain's coal producing districts and the number of mines electrified for the years 1913 and 1926

Coal producing district	Aggregate installed electrical horsepower (h.p.)		Percentage of total h.p. for GB	
	1913	1926[a]	1913	1926
Scotland	119,640	281,387	19.05	17.37
Northern	144,259	348,251	22.97	21.5
Yorkshire and north Midland	107,200	339,760	17.07	20.97
Lancashire, Cheshire and north Wales	30,718	94,094	4.89	5.81
South Wales	181,818	409,744	28.95	25.29
Midlands and Southern	44,435	129,985	7.07	8.02
Total h. p.	628,070	1,620,145[b]		

Notes:
[a] Figures for some of the districts differ from those given in the Annual Report, 1926, since in order to obtain a direct comparison with the MIR Returns, 1913, some regions have been regrouped.
[b] This is the total given in the *Annual Report*, 1926, and includes mines in Cleveland, Lincolnshire and Northamptonshire, but particulars are not given. The actual total for the above table is 1,603,221 h.p. The 1926 percentages are based on 1,620,145 h.p.

in 1887–88 at the Llanerch colliery, Monmouthshire, with A. T. Snell acting as the consulting engineer.[39] Then, in 1891 Snell was responsible for installing a sizeable electrical installation, at Crawshay Brothers' Newbridge Rhondda colliery, Pontypridd.[40] Here he used the recently developed compound wound d.c. generator in order to overcome the problems of excessive voltage drop created by the independent starting and stopping of pumps located some distance apart underground.

No doubt influenced by these early successes, a number of other colliery owners began installing electricity for lighting, pumping, haulage and miscellaneous applications. In 1897, under the direction of D. Selby Bigge, a contracting and consulting engineer from Newcastle,[41] Powell Duffryn installed d.c. generators manufactured by the Electrical Company, London, with the prime-movers being Nuremburg gas-engines utilising waste-gases from its Bargoed by-products plant, Also installed were one 60 kW, belt-driven d.c. generator and two pumps totalling 62 h.p. manufactured at the Close works of Ernest Scott & Mountain, Newcastle. In 1903 Bigge was able to state that he was responsible for installing more than 200,000 h.p. of generating capacity throughout Europe, which included 2,500 h.p. for Powell Duffryn, as well as a similar amount for the owners of Duffryn Rhondda colliery.[42]

Despite the willingness of an increasing number of colliery companies to venture into electrification, the d.c. systems were relatively small and confined mainly to lighting, the pumping of water, miscellaneous surface applications, for example screens and workshops, and the occasional underground rope haulage. The advent of large installations had to wait until the introduction of high-voltage, polyphase a.c. systems from about 1900. The choice of a.c. over d.c. was not on the grounds of safety, but because high-voltage a.c. transmission enabled

Table 2.3 (*Continued*)

Total number of mines and (%) electrified		Installed h.p. per mine		Installed h.p. per electrified mine	
1913	1926	1913	1926	1913	1926
319 (59)	343 (66)	221	542	375	822
272 (53)	257 (58)	285	791	530	1,355
320 (53)	286 (60)	168	209	335	1,188
131 (30)	141 (54)	71	331	234	667
294 (48)	363 (59)	299	671	618	1,129
152 (24)	169 (36)	82	275	337	769
1,501 (46)	1,559 (56)	192	570	418	1,029

Sources: Compiled from Mines Inspectors Reports, 1913, passim, and Annual Reports of the Secretary of Mines, 1926, p. 121

bulk supplies to be economically transmitted over much greater distances than was possible with d.c. However, the design and installation of high-voltage a.c. systems initially necessitated the expertise of experienced consulting engineers.

In 1902, the Tredegar Iron Company's (TICs) consulting engineer, Maurice Deacon, appointed Messers [Ernest] Scott & Mountain to supply and erect the first major three-phase system in South Wales,[43] although in 1903 W. A. Scott (of Scott & Legat, Cardiff)[44] stated that he was personally supervising the installation work. The electrical system, which was installed throughout a number of the collieries of TIC, had a total generating capacity of 1,150 kW. TIC's installed motor load of 950 h.p. would undoubtedly have been higher but for TIC's policy of prohibiting the use of electricity underground where fiery seams existed.[45] This practice was one that many colliery owners later adopted – and this persisted even after effective flameproof protection for electrical equipment had been proven.

There is little doubt that the installation of a three-phase plant of this size was an ambitious venture for the owners of TIC whose only previous experience of electricity was for d.c. lighting and local pumping. It certainly demonstrated the progressive nature of the company to opt for electricity rather than uprate the capacity of their compressed air plant in order to cope with the increasing output of coal (>1,100,000 tons annually in 1902). By 1905 the directors' of TIC were able to report on the success of this venture:

> ... their plant, the installation of which commenced four years ago, has now been working in its entirety for a sufficient period to enable the Directors to state, after exhaustive tests, minute enquiry, and comparisons, that the results fully justify the expenditure in adopting electricity as the motive power for hauling, pumping and lighting the collieries[46]

After this, TIC decided to extend their three-phase system.[47] In 1910 the decision was made to sink an all-electric pit at Markham, and from 1912 generating plant was either progressively installed or uprated at their various collieries, initially on an individual basis and, later, as part of an interconnected system so as to increase system integrity and reduce the capital and running costs. It is interesting to note that although Scott was appointed as TIC's resident engineer, probably after the success of the initial system and his ability was proven, he was allowed to undertake consultancy work for a number of other colliery companies, and later became a prominent figure in South Wales's engineering circles.

As TIC was installing their three-phase system, Powell Duffryn's plans to electrify their larger collieries in the Aberdare and Rhymney valleys was well in hand. Powell Duffryn's consulting engineer was C. P. Sparks, a high profile engineer whose early experience included manufacturing and pioneering work on electricity supply systems. He was also Chief Engineer to the County of London Electric Supply Company, as well as holding directorships of two other London electric supply companies. Sparks also performed notable work for the Institution of Electrical Engineers, not only writing and presenting journal papers, but also serving as Chairman of the Wiring Rules Committee (1900–15) and being one of the few men to be twice elected as the Institute's President (1915 and 1916).[48]

Sparks in 1884, at the age of eighteen, joined Ferranti, a pioneer of large-scale high voltage alternating current (a.c.) generation and transmission systems. Such was Sparks's ability that in 1887 he had become a partner with Ferranti and Ince. In the previous year Sparks was appointed engineer-in-charge of London's Grosvenor Gallery generating station,[49] following Ferranti's earlier appointment as chief engineer to resolve faults on the 1,200 V a.c. (later 2,400 V a.c.) installation. Ferranti (and, almost certainly, Sparks) identified fundamental faults including the replacing of the series connected transformers with ones of his own design and connected them in parallel (which is now standard practice), and realised the economies of scale that could be obtained from large capacity, high voltage alternating current (a.c.) generating plant.[50] Although the Grosvenor Gallery later closed, valuable experience had been gained in high voltage a.c. systems, experience that was soon put to good use in 1887 when Ferranti embarked upon the Deptford power scheme and proposed installing five alternators, each rated at 7,500 kW (more than ten times that of any alternator ever constructed) together with a 10,000 V distribution network.[51] Apart from difficulties with the manufacture of the alternators, Ferranti had to design cables capable of carrying these voltages since it was beyond the experience of cable manufacturers of the day. Additionally, he had to contend with increasing opposition from the supporters of low voltage d.c. systems (typically 220 V and 110 V) who believed that such high voltages were neither safe nor necessary. Ferranti, however, persevered, with Sparks assisting in the laying of these high voltage mains.[52] Even though problems were later encountered at Deptford, the advantages of high voltage a.c. transmission and the location of large-scale power stations in favourable positions were further reinforced, a pattern which Sparks, when he later became a consulting engineer, adopted in many of his schemes, including those of Powell Duffryn in South Wales.

The contract for all of Powell Duffryn's installation work in the Aberdare valley was awarded to the Electrical Company (of London) and work began in the Autumn of 1903 on a 3,000 kW, 50 Hz generating station at Middle Duffryn, with the Electrical Company providing both the supervising and resident engineers.[53] Later electrical work spread to the Rhymney valley, where Powell Duffryn's new pits were located. Capacity was increased regularly in both locations, with the Rhymney valley seeing generating stations being erected at the Elliot and Bargoed collieries in 1907 and the Penallta colliery in 1911.[54] The completion of the Penallta generating station provided sufficient electricity, together with a supply from Bargoed, to enable the nearby Britannia colliery to be sunk and operated entirely by electricity.[55]

The completion of Powell Duffryn's high voltage link in 1915 made its system the largest private colliery electrification scheme in Britain and one which was to become widely recognised as a 'model', both in terms of engineering excellence and with a low total cost of generating electricity (probably at less than 0.3d/unit),[56] attracting the attention of electrical engineers throughout Britain and overseas. In 1924 Powell Duffryn's generated output of 160.12 million units was to dwarf that of coalfield competitors such as the Ebbw Vale Iron & Steel Company (84.43 million units) and TIC (24.74 million units) and exceed the combined output of the four largest Statutory Undertakings in South Wales, namely those of Cardiff, Newport, South Wales Electric Power Company (SWEP) and Swansea, which stood at 129.3 million units.[57]

It is evident that Sparks and E. M. Hann, Powell Duffryn's General Manager and a prominent, progressive mining engineer himself, developed an early and good working relationship, one which was to continue for many years. Despite Sparks preparing the specifications, Powell Duffryn, like many other companies, worked on the basis of accepting the 'most favourable tender'.[58]

In 1919, upon the appointment of Major E. Ivor David as Powell Duffryn's chief engineer,[59] Sparks's involvement with the company ceased. Whether this was because Sparks, who had by now established a very successful engineering consultancy which boasted a broad-based international clientele, was unable to give the commitment which Powell Duffryn demanded, or whether the system had grown to such an extent that it became necessary to engage an experienced, full-time chief engineer, is not certain.

Whatever the reason, David, who prior to war service, had been, first, experimental and testing engineer to Brush, and then British-Thomson Houston's engineer and manager for South Wales and the west of England, proved himself to be a competent engineer enthusiastically promoting the interests of Powell Duffryn and colliery electrification in general.[60] Sparks, however, still continued to advise other colliery concerns in both the steam and the anthracite areas of the coalfield on electrical matters, some of which involved advising on the issue of the comparative costs between purchasing electricity externally from a Statutory Undertaking and that of self-generation.

Another high-profile engineer was W. H. Patchell, of the London-based firm of consulting engineers, who was retained by D. Davis & Sons for the electrification of their Ferndale collieries in 1908.[61] By 1913 Patchell was also acting as consulting engineer for John Lancaster & Company,[62] but his involvement here was probably due to D. Davis having acquired a financial interest in this concern. Given Patchell's earlier interest in SWEP and the fact that the Glamorgan Coal Company, the Cambrian Collieries and D. Davis & Sons all originally took their supplies from the 25 Hz lines of SWEP, it would not be unreasonable to assume that he, too, was their consulting engineer.

Being unable to fully understand the proposed changes in the structure of SWEP's tariff, the directors of Locket's Merthyr Collieries, in 1906, also turned to Patchell for advice.[63] Then, in early 1907 the same directors asked Sparks to advise upon self-generation.[64] Such an action was not one of choice, but from the real concerns of SWEP '... going to the wall'.[65] Locket's attitude to self-generation was extremely negative, with T. E. Richards clearly indicating that even if it was cheaper, '... let them [SWEP] have all the generating troubles'.[66] The prices subsequently obtained by Sparks for the proposed supply and erection of generating plant at Locket's Mardy colliery show wide variations, as Table 2.4 indicates, and perhaps indicate one of the advantages of obtaining a number of different tenders. Table 2.4 also shows that, all things being equal, British manufacturers were capable of successfully competing against their overseas counterparts.

In 1914 the directors of the Cynon Colliery Company instructed their consulting engineer, B. J. Day, of Cardiff, to prepare estimates for the supply and erection of a 1,200 kW generating station so that they could become independent of their suppliers, the neighbouring Duffryn Rhondda colliery, which had just been taken over by the Imperial Navigation Coal Company.[68] However, by 1919 both the Cynon and Duffryn Rhondda collieries had agreed to take a supply from the lines of the SWEP. Such a decision was, in all probability, the outcome of the action of Imperial Navigation's director, J. Andrews (who was also a director of SWEP) calling in W. A. Chamen, SWEP's manager, to advise on the best means of supply, given the increased requirements of the two concerns.[69]

Table 2.4 Summary of 'best tenders' for the supply and erection of proposed electrical generating plant at Locket's Merthyr Mardy colliery, 1907

Manufacturer	Basic price	Additional costs
Electrical Company	£9,618	
Siemens	£7,249	£25/10/0 per week labour, exclusive of travelling expenses of supervising engineer
British Westinghouse	£7,799	
Lahmeyer	£6,737	Plus (say) £600
Scott & Mountain	£5,599	Plus £600
Harland Bowden	£7,410	

Note: Rating of generating plant and details of ancillary plant, etc. not specified. However, in May 1907, Harland Bowden quoted Powell Duffryn a price of £8,367 for the supply and erection of a turbo-alternator rated at 2,000 kW.[67]
Source: GRO. D/D NCB 16/34 Agents Correspondence – Mardy Colliery. March 1906 – November 1907, entry dated 12 July 1907.

Other colliery companies known to have retained consulting engineers include the Ocean Coal Company, Aberpergwm Collieries and the Main Colliery Company, the latter two being in the anthracite region of the coalfield. The consulting engineer for the Ocean Coal Company was J. Samuels, later to be appointed vice-principal of the South Wales and Monmouthshire School of Mines.[70] J. Glynn Williams who was instrumental in forming the Association of Mining Electrical Engineers acted as consulting engineer for Aberpergwym, and C. P. Sparks advised the Main Colliery Company.[71]

As the growth of the use of electricity in the South Wales coal industry steadily increased (see Tables 2.2 and 2.3), ever increasing demands were being placed on a relatively small number of competent consulting engineers. One response was for some colliery companies to offer full-time employment to the consulting or installation engineer, as in the case of TIC and W. A. Scott. Although such engineers were still allowed to undertake consultancy work, their first priority obviously was to their employers, and on a large system this could mean little time for external commitments. Arguably, the filtering off of competent engineers in this way could deplete an already restricted supply, but it did have the benefit that these experienced engineers provided 'on-the-job' training to local labour to whom the day-to-day running of the plant could be entrusted. However, as installations increased in capacity and became more complex, some colliery owners realised that a higher level of expertise was needed. The answer to this came, coincidentally, by coal owners establishing their own School of Mines at Pontypridd and Crumlin, in 1913 and 1914 respectively.[72] Whilst these schools were established primarily for the training of mining engineers, the opportunity to train electrical and other technical staff could not be ignored. The funding for these two establishments was provided for by the participating coal owners donating a reported one-tenth of a penny (d) per ton of coal produced.[73]

After about 1920 an increasing number of colliery companies began engaging their own electrical engineers in favour of consulting engineers. Such men came from a variety of backgrounds, for example having been recruited from companies undertaking successful installations for consultants, having received 'on-the-job' training when working alongside consultants and/or installation engineers, having received further education and training at the Schools of Mines or other educational establishments, or by electrical personnel studying in their spare time to become certified members of the Association of Mining Electrical Engineers. Indeed, as time progressed, some of these men became consulting engineers in their own right.

Whilst there is every indication that the work done by consulting engineers, particularly for the medium-to-large colliery companies, was of good quality, problems did exist in the early years, as well indicated by W. A. Scott, in 1903, when he blamed many electrical failures upon)

> ... the advice of incompetent persons, and also that bugbear the lowest tender, which has much to answer for ...[74]

In 1910, Evan Williams, of Thomas William and sons, colliery owners, of Llangennech, when giving evidence to the Inquiry of the Use of Electricity in Mines, stated:

> ... the curse of electrical work at collieries has been in the competition between electrical firms and the cutting down of material.[75]

At the same Inquiry, B. J. Day, when asked as to the chief cause of accidents at mines, replied:

> ... that some people do not take any advice at all, they send out a general enquiry for plant, and there is very keen competition in these days for the work, with the result that people do not put forward what is the best installation.[76]

Evidently not all colliery owners were seeking advice from consulting engineers, but rather relying upon their own 'in-house' expertise or manufacturers to specify or supply equipment. This was an unsatisfactory state of affairs considering the concerns expressed by many observers about the low levels of 'in-house' expertise at both the 1903 and 1910 Inquiries into the Use of Electricity in Mines. Having then procured their equipment, such colliery owners involved these employees to install the equipment, leading to what Day described as '... scammed work'.[77]

One important role of the engineers (whether consulting or resident) employed by colliery companies was the need to develop a good working relationship with the equipment supplier. One reason for the high failure rates of colliery equipment and electrical plant, even as late as the 1930s, has been attributed to the poor design and construction at the manufacturing stage. If so, this suggests that the links between colliery engineers and the equipment engineers and designers were not always present or maintained. Day's earlier remarks clearly indicate the danger of relying purely upon the manufacturer's guidance. It is one thing for a piece of equipment to function perfectly well in a workshop on the surface of a colliery, but to expect its reliable and safe operation in the hostile conditions so often present underground is an entirely different matter. Where such links were developed, success was usually forthcoming. Powell Duffryn, for example, was actively involved in developing Sutcliffe's gate-end load and face machines, following a series of early failures. The success of this joint venture was such that by the First World War Powell Duffryn became Sutcliffe's biggest individual customer.[78]

5.4 Summary of the consulting engineer's role in the South Wales coal industry

Having examined the role of the consulting engineer in the South Wales coal industry and outlined some of the installations which they developed, the question which must now be answered is, in what way did consulting engineers play a positive part in the electrification of the south Wales coal industry, by way of contrast with the negative impact in respect of the ESI generally. First, it may be argued that circumstances were very much a controlling feature in that the decision to introduce electricity on a substantial scale was made by a very small number of colliery owners, namely those who could afford the high capital expenditure. This, together with the fact that those who were not able to afford such expenditure, had to await SWEP's slow development, meant that the widespread and possible uncontrolled proliferation of different schemes was prevented. Second, the consulting engineers retained were highly experienced and had proven technical ability, and many shared similar backgrounds or had worked together in the past. Third, it would appear that despite the undoubted ability of these consulting engineers, the colliery owners who engaged them ensured their accountability by vetting all communication and costings and procuring the equipment themselves, thus keeping costs as low as possible. Indeed, there is every indication that the resulting installations were very successful and acted as a stimulus to other colliery companies contemplating electrification. Powell Duffryn's installation, for example, was described by Merz himself as '... the most complete, certainly the largest system of colliery electrification in this country [Britain]'.[79] Indeed, Powell Duffryn's electrification was widely recognised as a 'model' system. Certainly Sparks (and David after him) enthusiastically promoted Powell Duffryn's electrification system and, no doubt, their own interests, through the pages of the publications of various learned bodies and societies, trade journals and the technical press.[80] Also, they actively encouraged visits from learned bodies and societies, and interested individuals, both from Britain and overseas.[81] Other colliery companies such as TIC, Ebbw Vale Iron & Steel Company and D. Davis, having early, large-scale electrification schemes adopted similar promotional activities. There is every indication that the knock-on effect of these successful, early, high-profile schemes, positively influenced other companies, generally throughout the British coal industry and overseas, contemplating the installation of electricity, in that they either based their schemes on these 'model' systems or engaged some of these consulting engineers themselves.

Finally, electrification would have still been introduced into the south Wales coal industry even if these high-profile and experienced consulting engineers had not been engaged at the time, as the commercial viability of high voltage, three-phase systems had just begun to emerge. However, if the more innovative and progressive colliery companies had not been careful in the selection of these consulting engineers, then it is highly likely that problems and unreliable systems would have resulted. This, in turn, would undoubtedly have had an adverse effect upon the rate of adoption of electricity within this particular industrial sector and, in all probability, in a wider context,

6 Conclusions

There seems little doubt that the views expressed by Saul, Aldcroft, Byatt, Hannah, Hughes and Wilson regarding the problems created by consulting engineers in the early days of the British electrical supply and manufacturing industry are largely correct. However, in defence of the consulting engineer, after about 1895 he was very much a victim of circumstance, in particular, those clients, primarily the LAs, who insisted upon the practice of accepting the lowest price tender. This practice, as we have seen, presented itself in two ways: first, that the consulting engineer would have been one of probably half a dozen people invited to submit a fee for agreeing to produce a report detailing the equipment needed together with the estimated costs, say, for the installation of an electricity generating plant. The engineer offering the lowest fee was normally engaged. Secondly, a similar constraint was then placed upon the consulting engineer, in that the costs appearing in his subsequent report was to reflect the lowest or best price obtained from a similar number of manufacturers. Usually the LAs would procure the equipment themselves, thereby eliminating any 'mark-up' by the consulting engineer and thus keeping the cost to the ratepayers to a minimum. But, of course, engaging one of the ever increasing numbers of consulting engineers, many of unproven experience, eager to offer their services in an expanding market and then insisting upon the manufacturer producing to the lowest price in a highly competitive market, does not always result in quality and reliable installations.

Other factors, both of a technical and legislative nature, further exacerbated the matter, such that by the early years of the Twentieth Century Britain's electricity supply network had become largely one of divergence. Nevertheless, positive benefits were obtained from the use of consulting engineers, particularly when close working relationships with equipment manufacturers were formed, the prime example being Merz with his pioneering work in the north-east.[82] Merz also undertook important work in South Wales when, in 1907, he was invited by SWEP's debenture shareholders to assess the state of the company and determine what steps were needed to stave off SWEP's imminent collapse.[83] Merz believed that a power scheme within South Wales was viable, provided that generation was focused upon one large, central generating station, instead of several small ones.

In seeking to establish whether similar difficulties were obtained in other industrial sectors, namely within the South Wales coal industry, this study has indicated that, whilst problems did exist, the use of consulting engineers at an early stage of electrification had many positive aspects. True, the conditions were different to that of the ESI in the sense that a.c. power equipment required lower system frequencies (as compared with lighting) and, hence, the scope for technical divergence was somewhat less, and secondly the initiative to implement electricity was initially very much the prerogative of a small, but growing number of medium-to-large colliery companies who were able to raise the high capital outlay needed for such a venture. Those in control of these companies took a responsible attitude from the outset and minimised the risks involved by drawing only from a small pool of high-calibre consulting engineers of proven experience and ability, and by ensuring their accountability. As in the case of the LAs, costs were kept to a minimum through the colliery owners/managers usually procuring the equipment themselves. Because of these measures a number of these electrification schemes quickly became 'model' systems and acted as an effective stimulus and guide to other colliery owners contemplating similar installations.

As time went on, more complaints seem to have been received regarding the poor quality of electrical equipment, particularly from the end-user perspective. Whilst some of these problems could well be attributed to manufacturers attempting to secure contracts in the face of intense competition and the widespread practice of lowest price tendering, other factors included the wider use of electricity and the increasing numbers of electrical engineers (particularly those now being employed 'in-house'), some having limited experience and expertise. This, in turn, would be reflected in low standards of expertise in the specification, installation and commissioning of plant. Although lying outside of the scope of this paper, considerable evidence exists to show that the failure rates of end-user equipment, in particular, in collieries, was often unacceptably high up to at least the early 1930s, perhaps demonstrating, in part, that the close working relationship so necessary between the manufacturer and the colliery electrical engineer (whether consulting or resident) was absent. Where close links between equipment manufacturers and consulting engineers existed, there is evidence that that equipment was much more robust and reliable.

Notes

ff

* In my PhD 'The introduction and development of electricity in the South Wales coal industry up to 1926' (Cardiff, 1999), the largely positive role which the consulting engineer played in the early development of electricity in the South Wales coal industry appeared to sharply contrast that of their counterparts in the electrical supply industry and elsewhere. Whilst it was outside the scope of the thesis to investigate this apparent anomaly, it clearly was a matter that demanded further attention. Hence the reason for this paper.

  I would also like to take the opportunity of thanking my supervisors Professor Hugh Bolton (Cardiff School of Engineering) and Dr Trevor

Boyns (Cardiff Business School) for their help and encouragement in completing my thesis.

1 Gwent Record Office (GwRO), A510R1/15, Report by E. Manville, 'The proposal to assist the Gas Works by the establishment of an electricity supply station', 28 April 1894.

2 I. C. R. Byatt, *The British Electrical Industry, 1875–1914* (Oxford, 1979), p. 177.

3 Glamorgan Record Office (GRO), D/D NCB 16/34 Agents Correspondence – Mardy Colliery. March 1906 – November 1907, entry dated 12 July 1907.

4 W. A. Scott, 'Electric motive power in mines and collieries' in *Proceedings of the South Wales Institute of Engineers,* Vol. XX11 (1903), p. 236.

5 G. M. Harvey, *Colliery Electrical Engineering* (London, 1928), p. 317.

6 Ibid., p. 31.

7 S. B. Saul, 'The American Impact on British Industry, 1895–1914' in *Business History*, Vol. 3 (1960), p. 20. In the same article, Saul quoted the following from *Engineering*, September 1896, p. 141: '... he [the consulting engineer] was more concerned in maintaining a reputation for infallibility (or for being different) than endeavouring to execute the work in the most economical manner. In short, money – other people's money – was no object'.

8 S. B. Saul, 'The Engineering Industry' in D. H. Aldcroft (ed.), *The Development of British Industry and Foreign Competition, 1875–1914* (Toronto, 1968), p. 231.

9 D. H. Aldcroft, 'Introduction: British Industry and Foreign Competition, 1875–1914' in
D. H. Aldcroft (ed.), *The Development of British Industry and Foreign Competition, 1875–1914* (Toronto, 1968), p. 35.

10 I. C. R. Byatt, *op. cit.* (1979), p. 177.

11 L. Hannah, *Electricity before Nationalisation* (London, 1979), p. 39.

12 T. P. Hughes, *Networks of Power* (1988, second printing), p. 120.

13 J. F. Wilson, *Ferranti and the British Electrical Industry, 1864–1930* (Manchester, 1988), p. 51.

14 J. F. Wilson, *British business history, 1720–1994* (Manchester, 1995), p. 94.

15 R. P. Sellon, 'The Standardisation of Electrical Engineering Plant' in *The Electrical Review*, 16 and 23 February 1900, pp. 287–8, 327–8.

16 Lt-Col Crompton's evidence given in Report and Minutes of Proceedings of the Committee on Electrical Legislation of the Institution of Electrical Engineers (1902), p. 31.

17 Ibid., pp 31–2.

18 The first comment was made by C. P. Sparks in 'Inaugural Address', *Journal of the Institution of Electrical Engineers (JIEE)*, Vol. 54 (1915), p. 1, and the second in discussion on 'The present position of electricity supply in the United Kingdom and the steps to be taken to improve and strengthen it', in *JIEE*, Vol. 54 (1916), p. 594.

19 Dafydd Tomos, The South Wales Story of the Association of Mining Electrical and Mechanical Engineers (Cardiff, 1960), p. 15.

20 S. F. Walker, 'On the principles of electric lighting and transmission of power by electricity, Section A – Electric lamps' in Transactions of the

South Wales Institute of Engineers (Trans. SWIE), Vol. X11 (1882–83), p. 116.

21 MacKechnie Jarvis, 'The generation of electricity' in *A History of Technology*, Charles Singer *et al.* (ed.), Vol. V (Oxford, 1958), p. 192.

22 T. P. Hughes, *op. cit.*, p. 171.

23 *Abergavenny Chronicle*, 9 March 1894, p. 3.

24 Alan Jones, 'The Old Chestnut: The introduction of electricity in Abergavenny', *Transactions of the Newcomen Society*, Vol. 72 (2000–2001), pp. 127–45.

25 For a summary of the development of the electrical supply industry up to 1926, see A. V. Jones, 'The introduction and development of electricity in the south Wales coal industry up to 1926'. Unpublished Ph.D. thesis (Cardiff, 1999), pp. 256–65.

26 A. V. Jones, *op. cit.* (1999), pp. 260–2.

27 *Report by the Electrical Trades Committee to the BoT*, 1917, cited in R. A. S. Hennessey, *The Electric Revolution* (Newcastle upon Tyne), 1972, p. 56.

28 L. Hannah, *op. cit.*, pp. 32 and 39. In 1905 the average price of electricity was 1.03*d.* per kWh.

29 C. P. Sparks, 'Electricity applied to mining', *JIEE*, Vol. 53 (1915), p. 389.

30 A. V. Jones, *op. cit.* (1999), pp. 356–60.

31 C. P. Sparks, *op. cit.*, Vol. 53 (1915), p. 389.

32 Ibid., p. 389 and Inspectors of Mines Report (1915).

33 T. Stretton, 'Presidential address to the Association of Mining Electrical Engineers', in *Mining Electrical Engineer (MEE)*, Vol. V1 (1925–26), p. 5.

34 S. F. Walker, *op. cit.*, p. 116.

35 *Ibid.*, p. 116.

36 W. Thomas, 'Electric lighting in collieries' in *Proc. SWIE*, Vol. X11 (1880–81), p. 570.

37 A. V. Jones and R. P. Tarkenter, *Electrical Technology in Mining: the dawn of a new age* (Stevenage, 1992), p. 32.

38 A. V. Jones, *op. cit.* (1999), pp. 226–7.

39 R. P. Tarkenter, 'The application of electricity in coal mining to about 1890, with a retrospective view from 1914', Unpublished MA thesis (Newcastle-upon-Tyne Polytechnic, 1983), p. 54.

40 A. T. Snell, 'Notes on electrical work in mines' in *Trans. SWIE*, Vol. XV11 (1890–91), pp. 196–8.

41 *Minutes of Evidence taken before the Departmental Committee on the Use of Electricity in Mines* (hereafter referred to as 1903 Inquiry), Cd 1917 (1904), QQ. 5999–6000.

42 *Ibid.*, App. 9, p. 215.

43 *Ibid.*, QQ. 4 and 4275.

44 W. A. Scott, *op. cit.*, p. 278. It has not been established whether W. A. and Ernest Scott was related.

45 *1903 Inquiry*, Q. 3589.

46 GRO, NCB D/D 16/35 – Agents Correspondence – Mardy Colliery, March 1906 – November 1907, entry dated 8 December 1906.

47 T. Stretton, *op. cit.*, pp. 6–7.

48 Obituary to C. P. Sparks, *JIEE*, Vol. 88, Part 1 (1941), p. 318.

49 *Ibid.*, p. 318.

50 J. F. Wilson, *op. cit.* (1988), p. 29.

51 I. C. R. Byatt, *op. cit.*, p. 102. Both the Grosvenor Gallery and Deptford power station have been well documented. Examples include: Kelvin Williams, 'Sebastian Ziani de Ferranti 1864–1930: Pioneer of electrical power systems' in *Electronics and Power*, August 1987, pp. 493–5; Kelvin J. Williams, 'A century in power: The history of Deptford power station' in *IEE Review*, February 1991, pp. 71–4; Brian Bowers, *A History of Electric Light and Power* (Stevenage, 1982), pp. 144–50 (Grosvenor Gallery and Deptford); Rob Cochrane, *Pioneers of Powers: The story of the London Electric Supply Corporation, 1887–1948* (published by London Electricity Board, 1987), pp. 9–15 (Grosvenor Gallery) and pp. 16–23 (Deptford); J. F. Wilson, *op. cit.* (1988), pp. 25–50.

52 Obituary, *op. cit.*, p. 318. The success of Ferrnati's 10,000 V cables was that they were still operating in 1933 when the lines were closed down. See Kelvin J. Williams, 'A century in power: the history of the Deptford Power Station' in *IEE Review*, February 1991, p. 72.

53 C. P. Sparks, 'Electrical equipment of the Aberdare collieries of the Powell Duffryn Company, *JIEE*, Vol. 46 (1906), pp. 477–98 and T. Boyns, 'The electricity industry in south Wales to 1949', *The Welsh History Review*, Vol. 15, No. 1 (1990), p. 84.

54 T. Boyns, *ibid.*, p. 84.

55 C. P. Sparks, *op. cit.*, Vol. 53 (1915), pp. 390, 403.

56 C. P. Sparks, *op. cit.* (1905), p. 498.

57 E. Garcke, *Manual of Electricity Undertakings*, Vol. XXX (1926–27), passim and T. Stretton, *op. cit.*, pp. 6–7.

58 GRO. D/D NCB 23, Powell Duffryn Minute Book No. 5, entry dated 11 December 1906.

59 Dafydd Tomos, *op. cit.* p. 24.

60 *Ibid.*, p. 24. Major E. Ivor David was an active supporter and contributor to a number of technical and learned societies, producing a number of papers based on the Powell Duffryn system. In 1927–28 he became Branch President for the Association of Mining Electrical Engineers and later became its National President. In 1927 David set up his own consulting practice.

61 Home Notes – Electrification of Collieries in *Journal and Proceedings of the South Wales Colliery Officials' Association*, June 1907, p. 4.

62 *Times Fuel Number*, reprinted from the issue of Monday, 1 December 1913 (1914), p. xliv.

63 GRO. NCB D/D 16/35, entry dated 26 July 1906.

64 *Ibid.*, entry dated 10 March 1907.

65 *Ibid.*, entry dated 21 January 1907.

66 *Ibid.*, entry dated 10 March 1907.

67 GRO. NCB D/D 23, entry dated 11 December 1906.

68 GRO. NCB D/D 22/11, Minute Books Imperial Navigation Coal Company Limited, entry dated 18 February 1914.

69 *Ibid.*, entry dated 22 December 1915.

70 Dafydd Tomos, *op. cit.*, p. 20.

71 G. H. Rutter, 'The electrification of the Main Colliery Company Limited, 1909, with analysis of nine years working', *Association of Mining Electrical Engineers*, Vol. X (1918–19), p. 77.

72 For the date of formation of the South Wales and Monmouthshire
    School of Mines (located at Treforest, Glamorgan) see: HEFCW Circu-
    lar W99/101/HE. http://www.wfc.ac.uk/education/hefcw/pub99/w99101he.
    html#annb (14.12.00), and for the Crumlin School of Mines (located at
    Crumlin, Monmouthshire), see: Introduction to Caerphilly. Where are
    we? http://www. caerphilly.gov.uk/where. html#crosskeys (12.12.00).
    Prominent electrical engineers had an input to these schools. In 1923, for
    example, Major E. Ivor David presented his paper 'Power Production at
    Collieries' to the South Wales and Monmouthshire School of Mines prior
    to its publication in the *MEE*. The purpose of the presentation was '...
    to show them [the students] that there was a field for them when they had
    completed their studies' *MEE*, Vol. 1V, October 1923, p. 143.
73 Dafydd Tomos, *op. cit.*, p. 8.
74 W. A. Scott, *op. cit.*, p. 236.
75 *Minutes of Evidence taken before the Departmental Committee Appointed
    to Consider the Working of the Existing Special Rules for the Use of Elec-
    tricity in Mines*, Cd 5533 (1911), Q. 3984.
76 *Ibid.*, Q. 6145.
77 *Ibid.*, Q. 6147.
78 Sutcliffe, Edward D., *Richard Sutcliffe: The Pioneer of Underground Belt
    Conveying* (1939), pp. 30–1.
79 C. H. Merz, on discussion in 'Electricity applied to mining', by C. P.
    Sparks, Vol. 53 (1915), p. 430.
80 For example, the following papers, either based on or referring directly
    to Powell Duffryn's electrification system, were published: C. P. Sparks,
    JIEE (1905 and 1915); E. I. David, *MEE* (1923 and 1926); *JIEE* (1925);
    Colliery Year Book and Coal Trades Directory (1923); *Institute of Fuel.*
81 For example, the following bodies, societies or organisations visited and
    inspected Powell Duffryn's electrification system at various times: Insti-
    tution of Electrical Engineers; South Wales Institute of Engineers; South
    Wales Colliery Officials' Association; Association of Mining Electrical
    Engineers (1912, 1913, 1921).
82 C. H. Merz has been the subject of a number of studies. Examples include:
    John Rowland, *Progress to Power: The contribution of Charles Merz and
    his associates to sixty years of electrical development, 1899–1959* (published
    for Merz & McLennan Ltd, 1960); The Pioneering Work of the Tyneside
    Electricity Industry. One-day conference held at Newcastle Upon Tyne, 26
    February 1994, by the Newcomen Society; A. Snow, 'Ferranti and Merz:
    power transmission design engineers' in *Engineering Science and Educa-
    tion Journal*, February 1998, pp. 5–10.
83 *The Electrical Review*, Vol. 59, 3 August 1906, pp. 188–9 (note: a shorter
    version of this article appeared in the *Western Mail*, 26 July 1906). *The
    Electrical Engineer*, Vol. 39, 11 January 1907, p. 64.

3 The British gas industry, 1949 to 1970

A regional comparison

Andrew Jenkins

1 Introduction

Nationalisation has always been a controversial subject and there has been a lengthy debate about the performance of the nationalised industries.[1] Opinions on the subject have varied but most commentators have tended to regard British public enterprise as inefficient, mainly because managers were severely hampered by problems of political interference.

A thorough enquiry by the Select Committee on Nationalised Industries, concluded in 1968, was highly critical of the way that relations between government departments and the nationalised boards had developed. Although the Select Committee acknowledged that the nationalised industries had achieved some successes, they argued that there was an underlying confusion about the responsibilities of government departments and the industries. While, in principle, Ministers were supposed to set out the broad lines of policy for the industries, but were not to become involved in the details of the implementation of policy, in practice the situation was almost the reverse of this. Ministers had provided very little broad guidance, but had become greatly involved in many aspects of management, including investment decisions, pricing policy and matters of staffing.[2]

The National Economic Development Office (NEDO) conducted a study in 1976 which produced similar results. There was a lack of trust and mutual understanding between the nationalised industries and those in government who were responsible for them. In particular the NEDO study pointed to the problem of reconciling the short-term perspectives of politicians with the longer time frames required for strategic decision-making in the nationalised industries. The framework for reaching agreement on long term objectives and strategies was not adequate, and managers were not confident that government

DOI: 10.4324/9781003331506-3

would provide them with the necessary continuity of policy.[3] A tendency towards ever more frequent interventions by government had 'delayed decisions, disrupted previously agreed plans, invalidated criteria for planning and assessing performance, resulted in financial deficits, and damaged the corporate morale of management and other employees'.[4]

The leading academic commentator on the nationalised industries in the 1960s and 1970s was Richard Pryke. In a major study of the first twenty years of nationalisation, published in 1971, he reached some very favourable conclusions about the performance of the nationalised industries, especially in the 1960s. Careful estimates showed that after a rather slow start in the first decade of public ownership, the productivity growth of the nationalised industries had been rapid between 1958 and 1968. Pryke attributed this improvement mainly to the system of financial targets for the industries which had been put in place by the government in the early 1960s. Tougher financial targets, it was argued, had put pressure on the nationalised industries to cut costs through higher productivity. Also important in rooting out bad practices and suggesting new methods were the scrutiny by the Prices and Incomes Board, and supervision of the industries by the sponsoring departments.[5]

However, in a follow-up study, covering experience from 1968 to 1978, he concluded that, generally the performance of the nationalised industries had been 'third rate, though with some evidence here and there of first class standards'.[6] The main culprits for this decline in performance standards were the various governments of the 1970s which had created confusion about the objectives of the industries and intervened arbitrarily in their affairs.[7]

As the movement towards privatisation gathered pace in the 1980s, economists stressed the uncompetitive business environment in which many of the nationalised industries had operated. It was argued that the industries had often faced little or no product market competition, were immune from stock market takeover threats and did not have the risk of bankruptcy to contend with. In such an uncompetitive environment poor management and inefficiency could survive unpunished.[8] Privatisation would impose market disciplines on the industries. A further advantage of privatisation was thought to be that it would weaken the ability of politicians to intervene in the management of the industries.

Economic and business historians, able to take a long-term perspective, have produced a more balanced and nuanced assessment of the nationalised industries' record.[9] Some historians have emphasised the very respectable productivity growth of the public enterprise sector, while acknowledging that its financial record was much weaker.[10] As historical work on the sector has accumulated it has become apparent that performance varied considerably from industry to industry in the nationalised sector.[11]

Nonetheless, historians have generally confirmed the finding of earlier commentators that government/industry relations were often a real source of difficulty. Changes in sectoral policies, such as energy policy, had harmful effects on the nationalised industries. For example, the electricity industry was constrained in its choice of feedstocks since the industry would have preferred a much smaller nuclear programme and a lesser role in the protection of the coal industry than was imposed on it by political pressures. The coal industry itself had to maintain uneconomic pits up to 1957, and thereafter, especially from the late 1960s, was run down at a very rapid rate.[12] Some industries were constrained in their choice of new technology by the 'technological nationalism' of politicians.[13] Macroeconomic interventions created delays and uncertainties for the pricing and investment plans of the nationalised industries throughout the post-war period, and these interventions probably became more frequent over time.[14]

In this paper, some new evidence on the performance of the nationalised gas industry is presented, by looking in detail at the record of two Area Gas Boards – the South Western and the East Midlands – in the 1950s and 1960s. Far less has been written about the nationalised gas industry than other nationalised industries such as electricity, coal and railways.[15] The evidence assembled here is used to test the robustness of some of the main hypotheses put forward about the nationalised industries by historians and other commentators. In particular, we look at the main factors which influenced the long-run strategies of the Gas Boards and at the business environments in which they operated. Did political interventions make long-run strategic planning difficult? How did the Boards formulate their strategies and what impact did the business environment have on them?

In order to address these questions, the experience of the two Area Boards needs to be considered in some detail. The remainder of the paper is divided into five sections. Section two supplies some background information on the gas industry and the Area Boards. It will be shown that there were great contrasts between the business environments in which the two Boards operated and together they can be seen as reflecting and representing many of the challenges and problems faced by the gas industry in the first twenty years after nationalisation. In section three a broad range of performance indicators are set out so that the achievements and weak points of the Boards can be clearly established. Sections four and five discuss the Boards' production and marketing strategies respectively, and the major influences which affected them. Finally, section six draws together the main conclusions, and assesses the implications of the findings for our understanding of the nationalised industries more generally.

2 The regions

The Gas Act of 1948 which transferred the gas industry to public ownership established a system of twelve Area Boards, each responsible for gas supply in its own region. The main duties of the Area Boards under the 1948 Act were 'to develop and maintain an efficient, co-ordinated and economical system of gas supply for their area'. The Gas Council was much weaker than the central bodies in the other nationalised industries. The Area Boards set their own tariffs, prepared their own plans for production and marketing, and submitted their capital programmes direct to the Minister. The programmes were approved by the Minister after consultation with the Gas Council.[16] The Area Boards were also financially autonomous. They were each expected to break even taking one year with another.[17] It was not until the late 1960s that the position of the Gas Council was strengthened. With the onset of North Sea gas it acquired powers to manufacture and distribute gas, and to plan and co-ordinate the development of the industry. This gathering of power to the centre was completed by the 1972 Gas Act which established the British Gas Corporation.

There were variations between the Area Boards both in the size and composition of demand for gas, and in the ease of access to raw materials with which to manufacture and supply it. The differences between the East Midlands and the South Western Boards were particularly marked.

The area of the South Western Gas Board (SWGB) covered 8,400 square miles and was some 250 miles in length.[18] It included Cornwall, Devon, Somerset, Bristol, and Gloucestershire, as well as small parts of other counties such as Wiltshire, Oxfordshire and Warwickshire. The region was sparsely populated, with much agricultural land and relatively low levels of urbanisation.

The territory of the East Midlands Gas Board (EMGB) was more compact at some 6,400 square miles, and covered the eastern side of England between the Humber and the Wash. Thus, the area included South Yorkshire and South Humberside which would not today be regarded as part of the Midlands. In general the region was more urbanised and industrial than the South West, with extensive coalfields and metal-working areas.

The population of the East Midlands was 4.6 million in 1949, compared to only three million within the South Western region.[19]

The East Midlands Board also had more gas customers than its South Western counterpart. In the early years of public ownership, in 1951, the East Midlands Board had almost a million domestic consumers, while the South Western Board had about 600,000. The main contrast between the markets of the two Boards, however, was in terms of the composition of demand.

From Table 3.1 it can be seen that the domestic and commercial markets of the two Boards were reasonably comparable in size, but the East Midlands had a huge industrial market in addition, which made its aggregate sales nearly three times as large as in the South West. The East Midlands Board accounted for nearly 20 per cent of the total industrial demand for gas in the country as a whole, while the South Western Board had only about two per cent of the national industrial market.

There were differences between the Boards on the supply side. In the early years of public ownership the gas industry continued to rely on coal as its basic raw material. The majority of the Area Boards drew most of their gas supplies from coal gas manufactured in their own works, supplemented by carburetted water gas (CWG), which made use of the coke which was a by-product of carbonisation and was the traditional means of producing gas at short notice to meet peak loads. Nationally, in the financial year 1950/51, some 71 per cent of supplies were manufactured by the Boards by coal carbonisation, with a further 14 per cent obtained as CWG (see Table 3.2). The East Midlands, along with a few other Boards, purchased a sizeable proportion of its supplies in the form of coke oven gas, and was thus less reliant on manufacture than most other Boards. The South West relied on

Table 3.1 The Market for Gas, 1959/60, by Sector and by Area Board. Thousand therms.

	East Midlands	*South Western*	*Great Britain*
Domestic	113,528	66,594	1,267,825
Industrial	156,653	18,968	818,647
Commercial	28,477	18,273	386,034
other	7,698	4,439	118,301
Total Gas Sold and Used	306,356	108,274	2,590,807

Source: Gas Council Annual Report, 1959/60, Appendix III.

manufacture for 100 per cent of its gas supplies, having no sources of purchased gas in the region.

It would seem then, that in terms of business environment, most of the advantages were with the East Midlands Board. On the demand side it had a more densely populated area and larger average sales per customer, compared to the South Western Board, while on the supply side, the East Midlands had a wider variety of sources of gas to draw upon.

3 Measuring performance

In this section we present performance indicators for the two Area Boards. The tasks of each Board included the manufacture of gas, and the selling of by-products and gas appliances. They had to choose the most appropriate technology, manufacture and distribute gas efficiently, keep costs under control, market their products effectively and meet their financial obligations. Therefore, we need a broad range of indicators which reflect these diverse activities and so enable a balanced assessment of each Board's overall performance to be made. Fortunately, statistics are available, compiled by the Gas Council, to enable this to be done. The statistics will be used to examine, firstly, the production activities of the Boards and the speed with which they took advantage of technological change, then their financial results, and, finally, sales performance.

Table 3.2 Proportions of gas made and gas bought, 1950/51, per cent

	East Midlands	South Western	All Boards
Gas Manufactured:			
Coal Gas	40.89	81.89	71.01
Carburetted Water Gas	9.67	16.54	13.93
Blue Water Gas	0.37		0.89
Producer, Oil and Other Gases	0.37	1.57	1.93
Total Gas Manufactured	51.30	100.00	87.76
Gas Bought:			
Coke Oven Gas	48.70		11.97
Oil Refinery Gas			0.27
Total Gas Bought	48.70		12.24
Total Gas Available:	100.00	100.0	100.00

Source: Gas Council Annual Report, 1950/51.

During the 1950s and especially in the 1960s, new technology and diversification of supply had, together, brought about a great reduction in the proportion of total output which the Boards manufactured by the traditional coal-based methods. Table 3.3 reveals the extent to which the Boards had changed by 1966/67.

Nationally, less than a third of aggregate supplies now came from coal gas manufacture, and the industry was drawing on oil gas, liquefied petroleum gas, and imported natural gas from Algeria. At the regional level, the East Midlands continued to buy in a sizeable amount of coke oven gas, but it was also taking advantage of the new sources of supply. The technological path adopted by the South Western Board was highly unusual in two respects. Firstly, it was less diversified than other Boards, and, secondly, it continued to manufacture a very high proportion of its total output from the traditional coal-based carbonisation process. However, coal usage did fall sharply at the very end of the 1960s, as the South West belatedly came into line with the rest of the industry.

Some information on labour productivity, measured as value-added per employee, is presented in Table 3.4. It shows that the South Western Board achieved impressive levels of value-added per employee, especially in the 1950s. Of the twelve Area Gas Boards, the SWGB had only the ninth highest productivity level in 1949, but had improved its ranking to second by 1954 and maintained this position up to, and

Table 3.3 Gas made and gas bought, 1966/67, per cent

	East Midlands	South Western	All 12 Boards
Gas Made			
Coal Gas	22.04	65.86	28.02
Oil Gas	28.44	26.65	27.99
Other Gas Made	4.60	4.86	7.98
Total Gas Manufactured	55.09	97.37	63.99
Gas Bought and Reformed:			
From other Area Boards	0.08	–	0.03
From Coke Ovens	32.90	–	9.95
Refinery Gas	–	–	7.53
Liquefied Petroleum Gas	4.47	2.64	10.89
Imported Natural Gas	6.07	–	6.46
Other	1.39	–	1.16
Total Gas Bought and Reformed	44.91	2.64	36.01
Total Gas Available	100.00	100.01	100.00

Source: Gas Council Annual Report, 1966/67.

including, 1960/61. During the 1960s its relative level of value-added per employee fell back a little but it remained among the best in the industry. The EMGB had one of the lowest levels of labour productivity by this measure, ranking second last by 1954. It then improved to take a place in the top half of the league table up to 1966/67, before slipping to ninth by 1968/69. Overall, then the South Western Board's labour productivity was impressive, while the East Midlands Board tended to vary between poor and average.

However, information on costs puts the East Midlands Board in a more favourable light than the South Western. Figure 3.1 shows the trend of unit costs over the period. It is clear that costs in the South West were well above average, while the East Midlands Gas Board's costs were consistently below average.

Next, we assess the financial results of the Boards. Figure 3.2 shows the surpluses earned by the East Midlands and South Western Boards as a proportion of their turnover in each year. The surpluses earned were quite small: never more than five per cent of turnover, and often less than two per cent. The South Western Board made a large loss in its first year of trading, and fell into deficit in several other years during the 1950s, while the East Midlands Board was generally in surplus, apart from one year towards the end of the 1960s.

While the nationalisation statutes generally specified that Boards had to break even taking one year with another, financial targets were tightened in the early 1960s. The targets required the Boards to earn a specified rate of return on average net assets over the five year period beginning with the financial year 1962/63 and ending in 1966/67. The targets varied from Board to Board according to their differing circumstances. The industry as a whole narrowly missed the target set for it, and this was also true of both the South Western and East Midlands Boards (Table 3.5).

Table 3.4 Ranking of value added per employee, from 12 Area Boards, 1949 to 1968.

Area Board	1949	1954	1959/60	1960/61	1966/67	1968/69
East Midlands	6	11	6	4	4	9
South Western	9	2	2	2	6	4

Sources: For 1949 to 1959/60, Gas Council Annual Return to the Ministry of Power, 1959/60, Public Record Office POWE 43/166; for 1960/61 and 1966/67, Gas Council Report on Productivity, 1967, SWGB Chairman's Committee Reports, Oct. 1967, National Gas Archive BG31/SWO/CC/AM29; for 1968/69, SWGB Chairman's Committee Reports, Oct. 1969, National Gas Archive BG31/SWO/CC/AM31.

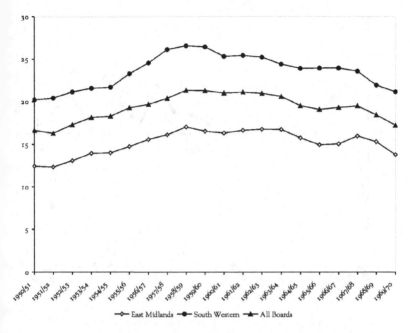

Figure 3.1 Area Boards' total unit costs in 1960 prices, old pence (d) per therm.

Surveying the financial indicators as a whole, there was perhaps not a great deal to choose between the two Area Boards, although the South West was more prone to falling into deficit.

Finally, we examine the sales records of the Boards. Table 3.6 shows that the number of customers in the South West was in decline, while the East Midlands had a rising number of customers.

The growth of gas sales per domestic consumer was also poor in the South West, and much more impressive in the East Midlands (Table 3.7). In 1950, gas sales per domestic consumer were relatively high in the South West but low in the East Midlands. All Boards saw a downward trend in sales per domestic consumer in the 1950s, but the East Midlands experienced rapid growth in the 1960s, while growth in the South West was very poor when placed against the benchmark of average performance across the whole industry.

Declining numbers of consumers and poor growth in sales per consumer implied that the growth of total sales would be poor for the South West, and this is confirmed by the data in Table 3.8. The

42   *Andrew Jenkins*

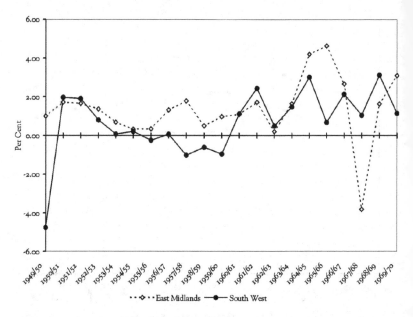

Figure 3.2 Area Boards' ratio of surplus to turnover, 1949/50 to 1969/70.

Table 3.5 Average gross return on average net assets, 1962/63 to 1966/67

	Target set, per cent	Results achieved, per cent
East Midlands	10.4	10.2
South Western	9.8	9.5
All Boards	10.2	9.8

Sources: Gas Council Annual Reports, and Area Board Annual Reports, 1966/67.

Table 3.6 Total number of consumers, by Area Board

Area Board	1950/51	1955/56	1960/61	1965/66	1970/71
East Midlands	1,054,481	1,155,569	1,219,647	1,272,829	1,318,621
South Western	623,787	656,074	635,015	613,487	594,208
All Boards	11,981,107	12,792,207	12,831,707	12,932,737	13,371,780

Source: Gas Council Annual Reports. Number of Consumers at end financial year.

Table 3.7 Average gas consumption per domestic consumer, by Area Board, therms

Area Board	1950/51	1955/56	1960/61	1965/66	1970/71
East Midlands	110.1	101.5	105.7	174.2	322.9
South Western	134.0	117.2	110.7	130.8	211.5
All Boards	124.4	112.7	106.5	164.5	286.6

Source: Calculated from Gas Council Annual Reports.

Table 3.8 Average annual growth rate of total sales, per cent, by Area Board, and compared to the national average

	East Midlands	*South Western*	*Great Britain***
1950/51 to 1957/58	2.66	–0.58	1.07
1957/58 to 1964/65	4.07	0.84	2.81
1964/65 to 1970/71	11.11	8.88	10.12

*Excluding direct sales by the Gas Council.
Source: Calculated from Gas Council Annual Reports.

East Midlands Board, on the other hand, consistently achieved sales growth at a rate well above the national average.

As well as gas, the Boards also sold by-products and appliances such as cookers. To take account of these broader aspects of sales performance each Board's share in total gas industry turnover was examined. The East Midlands' share of industry turnover was about seven per cent at the beginning of the period, and it had risen to almost ten per cent by the late 1960s. The South West, on the other hand, saw its share of industry turnover diminish from roughly six per cent in the early 1950s to some 4.5 per cent by 1970.

On sales performance, then, whichever indicator we select, the East Midlands emerges as a strong performer during this period, while the South West was among the weakest in the gas industry.

Overall, there were clearly major differences in the performance of the two Boards. The East Midlands had a low cost base, seems to have moved rapidly to take advantage of the new technological opportunities, and was able to achieve a high rate of sales growth. The South West, on the other hand, appears to have been a technological laggard, with high costs and very poor growth of sales. But its productivity record was much more impressive than that of the East Midlands. In the following sections of this paper, we seek to explain these contrasts by looking at the production and marketing strategies of the two Boards in some detail.

4 Production

The Heyworth Report of 1945, which preceded nationalisation, had argued that there were far too many small and inefficient gasworks operating throughout the country.[20] During the 1950s the Area Boards each developed and implemented plans for integrating production in their regions, concentrating on the improvement of the larger works and closing down small and obsolete plants. Starting with over 100 works each at vesting date in 1949, both the East Midlands and South Western Boards had cut the number of works to around 30 by 1960.[21] Efficiency gains accrued as a result.[22]

Unfortunately, the realisation of scale economies in production did not guarantee the future prosperity of the gas industry since other costs were rising rapidly. During the 1950s gas coals were rising in price, and generally at a faster rate than the raw materials used by rival fuel industries.[23] New production methods were urgently needed.

The gas industry responded by exploring the potential of several new processes. Among these were an ambitious scheme to import liquefied methane from Algeria which was delivering some ten per cent of Britain's gas requirements by 1966.[24] In close collaboration with the NCB the gasification of cheaper grades of coal was also explored (the Lurgi process). Two commercial scale plants were built but the process did not turn out to be viable.[25]

By the early 1960s it was becoming apparent that the best future for the gas industry lay in reforming light fractions of oil.[26] In 1962 research by ICI on producing a cheap source of hydrogen for the manufacture of ammonia bore fruit. The new process produced a lean gas by the steam reforming of light distillate feedstock in the presence of a catalyst. The potential of the new process was quickly realised by the gas industry and was complemented by ongoing Gas Council research on the manufacture of rich gases which could be mixed with the ICI steam reformer to produce town gas. These new methods proved to be sufficiently cheap to oust coal carbonisation as the favoured method of town gas production during the 1960s. Light distillate feedstocks were inexpensive, the processes required little labour, and the capital costs were a fraction of those for carbonisation plant, perhaps 1d to 1.2d per therm in the mid-sixties, compared to 6.5d for carbonisation.[27] So, even before any discoveries were made in the North Sea, the gas industry had a range of new sources of gas and new processes of manufacture to which it could turn for the reduction of its costs and the rejuvenation of its fortunes in the marketplace. We shall now examine how the Area Boards in the South West and the East Midlands chose to make use of the new opportunities.

The background to production strategy in the South Western Board in the late 1950s was one of cost problems and financial pressures. Because of its distance from the coalfields, the cost of transporting coal to the region was very high. The unit costs of meeting its debt and interest obligations also tended to be much higher than the industry average.[28] As a result, the Board's strategy was dominated by cost-cutting. For example, its workforce was cut back much more aggressively than the average for the industry as a whole, as shown in Table 3.9.

But, in the late 1950s, despite reductions in the size of the labour force and other savings from its integration programme, the Board began to drift into deficit as gas sales declined and by-product sales slumped (see Figure 3.2).

Although the Board Chairman, C. H. Chester, played down the significance of the deficits in public, the archival evidence clearly shows that, in private, the members of the Board were deeply concerned about the financial problems. They were fearful for their autonomy and for their jobs if the situation was not turned round, suspecting that, 'the continuance of results like this could only have one ultimate result, namely, the taking over of the Board by the Gas Council'.[29]

By late 1959, the SWGB was faced with the prospect of a third successive year in deficit and was looking with great urgency for ways of reducing costs. Negotiations were opened with the National Coal Board and the British Transport Commission with a view to obtaining a reduction in the total cost of the Board's coal supplies. Agreement was reached very speedily with the NCB on a five year coal contract, beginning in July 1959. The South Western Board agreed to take 1,200,000 tons of coal per annum (plus or minus five per cent). In return the NCB offered a reduction of five shillings per ton off the normal pit price of coal supplied.[30] A new contract with the railways offered additional savings.[31]

The SWGB derived short-term benefits from the contracts. They gave the Board 'a breathing space', freed it from pressing financial

Table 3.9 The size of the labour force of the area gas boards

	East Midlands	South Western	All boards
1950/51	10,388	8,760	143,506
1955/56	11,112	7,661	141,713
1960/61	9,920	6,068	124,259
1965/66	10,101	6,444	121,497
1970/71	10,684	5,686	114,768

problems.[32] The reductions in the cost of buying and transporting coal were substantial. In 1958/59 the Board had spent £8.1 million on coal (including transport costs). In 1959/60 this fell to only £7.2 million, albeit for a marginally lower tonnage.[33]

However, by agreeing to take 1.2 million tons per annum from 1959 to 1964 the South Western Board was committing itself to not reducing the amount of coal gas it would make at all over the ensuing five years. Should any new processes become available during this time the Board could only make use of them to meet peak loads or additional demands.[34] As the new processes swept through the industry from 1962 onwards the SWGB found its coal contract increasingly burdensome.[35]

The technological opportunities in the South West were quite limited. The Board did not have access to supplies of bought-in gas, nor was it one of the Area Boards which were able to take imported Algerian natural gas.[36] Moreover, its geographical location meant that it was one of the last Boards to receive supplies from the North Sea.[37] For most of the 1960s the South Western Board's choices were essentially between cheap oil gas and relatively expensive gas obtained from the coal carbonisation process.

The SWGB was actually one of the pioneers of the oil gas process, with its first plant, at Avonmouth, beginning production in late 1964. However, the plant could not be fully utilised because coal carbonisation plant had to be used for base load, so that the new plant was largely confined to meeting peak loads in its early years of operation. A report prepared by the Chief Engineer, in 1962, had predicted that a 20 million cubic feet per day reforming plant installed at Avonmouth then, with the NCB contract in place, it could only be used to a limited extent to produce about 12 million therms per annum at a cost of 10.2*d*. per therm (including capital charges). But, if the Board was able to shut down some of its carbonising plant, and operate the reformer on base load, then it could produce 34 million therms at a cost of only 7.21*d*. per therm.[38]

Although the five-year coal contract ran only until 1964, the SWGB was unable to escape easily. If the Board's take of coal dipped much below 1.2 million tons it would have had to pay an extra five shillings per ton on the whole amount of coal used by it. The Board could not shift suddenly to using no coal, and a gradual rundown below 1.2 million tons per year would be extremely costly. In negotiations, the NCB pressed for a ten year extension of the contract and would not accept any reduction in the tonnage taken. The SWGB was forced into renewing the contract for a further five years.[39] For virtually the whole of the 1960s, the Board was prevented from adopting new technology at the speed which it would have preferred. Fortunately, however, some re-negotiation of the contract was achieved during 1966/67. The SWGB were willing to offer to continue taking some coal after 1969, in return for a progressive rundown of coal supplies from 1967/68 onwards. This would enable them to phase out their coal carbonising plant in a measured, rather than abrupt, fashion. Negotiations continued for some time and an agreement was reached in March 1967.[40] The outcome gave the SWGB more leeway in the last year or 18 months of the contract, allowing the closure of coal carbonising plant to be accelerated and the tonnage of coal reduced.[41] This reduced some of the problems caused by the coal contract, but it had undoubtedly prevented the Board from moving as fast as it would have liked towards the new oil-based technology. Eventually, however, the Board was able to increase capacity at Avonmouth in the latter 1960s and also to construct a second oil reforming plant at Plymouth.

The situation in the East Midlands was very different from the South West. Here the Gas Board was much more favourably placed in terms of its access to a variety of methods of obtaining its gas supplies. During the 1950s the EMGB had relied increasingly on the purchase of coke oven gas, both from the NCB and from various private sector steel and chemical companies. Coke oven gas supplies had expanded from 25 million cubic feet in 1950/51 to 39 million cubic feet by 1957/58, and from about 45 per cent of all gas supplied by the Board to some 59 per cent over the same period.[42] The East Midlands Board's costs were among the lowest in the industry, and this had contributed to its success in increasing the demand for gas in the region. In contrast to the cost-cutting measures introduced of necessity in the South West, the emphasis at East Midlands was on getting sufficient capacity in place to meet the rising trend of demand.

From the end of the 1950s, following several years of depressed trade in the coke market, the NCB and other suppliers of coke oven gas began to close down some of their ovens. The rate of decline in the availability of coke oven gas was fairly gentle because contracts had to be worked to their conclusion but in the long run this meant that the EMGB had to move towards other sources of supply.[43] Coal carbonisation in the Board's own works was also in sharp decline during the 1960s. Unconstrained by coal contracts, the Board was able to implement a programme of works closures. Production by this method fell from 125 million therms in 1964/65 to 43 million therms five years later.[44]

The Board needed to replace out-moded techniques and to meet growing demands for its product. Capital was allocated to several ambitious projects. The Board was involved in the scheme to import liquefied methane from Algeria from an early stage and it was one of the seven Area Boards which confirmed their commitment to the scheme towards the end of 1960.[45] The EMGB planned to take some 36 million therms per annum.[46]

The Board also planned to make use of the new oil plants. One was ordered for Sheffield, which began production in 1964. This was complementary to the Algerian methane project since the methane could be utilised to enrich the gas made by the ICI steam reformer. A large new works was constructed at Killingholme, on the south bank of the Humber, near Grimsby. Having a works near the coast offered significant economies over delivering feedstock to inland plants, and Killingholme was well-located for supplies of feedstock arriving from Immingham docks, and new oil refineries were planned for the area.[47] The first stage produced town gas by reforming light petroleum distillate and enriching it with butane, and had a capacity of 50 million cubic feet per day (mcfd). Two further stages were then planned, taking capacity to over 150 million cubic feet per day. These came into operation between 1964 and 1967, by which time a further stage was needed.[48] Other reforming plants were constructed at Northampton, with a capacity of 100 mcfd, and at Ambergate, near Derby, which had a capacity of 145 mcfd. Both of these plants also made use of Algerian methane off the national pipeline, as the cheapest method for enrichment.

Because of its geographical location, the East Midlands Board was involved in taking North Sea gas from the earliest stage. The gas from BP's field in the North Sea was delivered to a shore terminal north of the Humber, and then piped to the East Midlands' Killingholme works for reforming into town gas.[49] The first supplies began to flow through the national pipeline in July 1967.[50]

It was planned that the intake of natural gas should first be absorbed into the existing manufacturing and distributing system (i.e. by using it to make town gas), then that direct supplies could be given to industrial consumers in Sheffield, followed by the task of converting the whole of the Board's distribution system to natural gas.[51] Because there was a separate grid system in Sheffield for industrial customers, it was convenient to convert this to natural gas at an early stage. Burton-on-Trent was selected as the first town to be wholly converted to natural gas (initially Algerian methane rather than gas from the North Sea), to provide practice because it was relatively small (around 20,000 customers), and because it was near to the national methane pipeline.[52]

Over the following few years these plans were put into effect. Conversion began at Burton-on-Trent in May 1967 followed by other towns and villages in the Board's area, and work started on the conversion of Sheffield industry in March 1968. By the end of March 1970 some 240,000 customers had had their appliances converted and natural gas sales represented almost a quarter of gas sold by the Board. Teams of contractors were moving steadily through other parts of the East Midlands, changing customers over to natural gas at the rate of 5,000 per week.[53] The East Midlands was at the forefront of a massive transition to natural gas. By this stage, conversion had begun all over the country, and this huge task was to be successfully accomplished by the mid-1970s.

The East Midlands was clearly in a fortunate position, compared to other Boards, in terms of its access to a range of relatively cheap sources of gas supply. It made the most of these advantages. The South Western Board was in a very difficult situation for most of the 1950s and 1960s. However, it added to its problems by locking itself into a long-term coal contract.

5 Marketing

In the early 1950s there were shortages of steel and other materials as well as restrictions on marketing in the form of hire purchase, advertising and taxation policies. In this environment it was not surprising that the Boards did not pursue active selling policies. Other industries, such as electricity, were also subject to similar restrictions, and there is little doubt that competition in the fuel sector became more intense in the latter part of the 1950s, as many of these constraints eased.[54]

The three main markets in which the gas industry competed were domestic, industrial and commercial. Industrial and commercial consumers were highly price-sensitive, and as the price of gas relative to those of its competitors, oil and electricity, was rising throughout the 1950s, growth prospects for the gas industry were very limited in both these sectors.[55]

Uncompetitive prices also hampered the gas industry in the domestic sector but here growth prospects were better. In the 1950s the standard of warmth and comfort in most homes was very low. Various studies showed that, for many consumers, a good standard of heating was only provided in one room of the house, and that other parts of the house lacked sufficient background heating to allow the occupants to move from room to room in comfort.[56] It was estimated that in 1956 some 98 per cent of households depended on solid fuel for their main space heating.[57] At this time, insofar as gas was used at all for space heating, its use was supplementary and on a very small scale. From the late 1950s, there was a rising demand for domestic space heating products. Gas appliance manufacturers began to develop better kinds of gas heater to meet this demand. Moreover, the poor image of gas – as smelly and old-fashioned – was addressed by the Gas Council which commissioned a series of very successful advertising campaigns from 1963 onwards.[58]

In the East Midlands, there was a very swift response to the new opportunities offered in the market for domestic space heating in the late 1950s. The Board's tariff structure had gradually become more promotional during the course of the decade, and a new two-part tariff for domestic consumers was introduced in 1957, with the objective of stimulating increased consumption levels.[59] Advertising by the East Midlands Gas Board aimed to demonstrate, for instance, that central heating was cheaper to install and cheaper to run than a similar oil-based system. The Board was also at pains to point out that 'East Midlands gas is cheaper than in most other parts of the country'.[60] New showrooms were opened and existing ones improved. Dealers in kitchen equipment and household goods were encouraged to stock gas appliances with the incentive of commission on any sales concluded.[61]

But the most important new development was that substantial numbers of 'special salesmen' began to be recruited and trained. The idea was that they should go out to make contact with the public rather than being tied to a showroom and would be able to spend the whole of their work time devoted to selling appliances, free from the administrative and other tasks which hampered the sales efforts of conventional sales and service staff.[62] At this time, the idea of employing salespeople in this way was very innovative.

The sales effort of the East Midlands Board quickly bore fruit, aided by the relaxation of hire purchase restrictions which occurred in October 1958. It was estimated that in 1957 there were about 205,000 gas fires in use in the East Midlands Board's Area. Over the next five years some 167,000 fires were sold, of which only 10,000 were replacement sales. The East Midlands' gas space heating load, which had accounted for only four per cent of the total domestic load in 1957/58, was taking some 22.5 per cent of the domestic load by 1961/62.[63]

However, such success created problems of its own. By early 1962, it was becoming apparent that supply was having difficulty in keeping pace with the rising demand for gas. During severe weather conditions in December 1961 and January 1962 it was reported that, 'outputs such as those experienced have put a tremendous strain on the Board's production capacity'.[64] There was no doubt that it was space heating sales which were causing such large peak demands. It was necessary to rein in the efforts of special salesmen, at least as far as space heating appliances were concerned. The Board decided not to advertise gas fires and central heating equipment. The EMGB switched its selling effort to gas cookers and water heaters, all year round loads which would not generate adverse seasonal peaks.[65] The policy of concentrating on the cooking and water heating loads and allowing space heating merely to develop under its own momentum because of the supply situation continued for several years.[66] As supply constraints eased in the late 1960s, the Board began to sell space heating appliances and central heating more enthusiastically.

In sharp contrast to the mood of expansion in the East Midlands in the late 1950s, the South Western Board was experiencing severe financial difficulties. Although many gas boards were putting sales drives into effect at that time the need for efficiency savings and cutbacks took priority over the opportunities for sales growth in the South West. In July 1958, the Chairman announced that budget cuts of £200,000 per annum were needed. As part of this cost-cutting exercise, publicity expenditure was reduced from about £105,000 in 1957/58 to only £65,000 in 1958/59.[67] This was very unfortunate timing since it coincided with a relaxation of hire purchase restrictions.

Further cuts in expenditure followed. In October 1960 it was decided that the total number of employees should be cut back by 395 by March 1962. Nearly half of this reduction was to be effected in the consumer service department.[68] Although there were no further cuts in publicity expenditure after 1958, and the manpower reductions within consumer services left the numbers of sales and service staff unscathed, yet there was clearly no scope for expansion.

On several occasions the SWGB Chairman called for sales drives but extra resources were not put in place to back up this desirable objective.[69] Higher sales had to be achieved by intensification of effort by existing sales staff and there was a limit to what could be accomplished by such means. Sales staff were also hampered by administrative and other duties. In 1959 the Area Development Manager reported that district sales and service managers were spending more time than they should on clerical matters, while outdoor sales staff spent as much as one-third of their time on ancillary duties, rather than direct sales.[70]

The South Western Board may also have been slow to appreciate that opportunities were available in the domestic space heating market. At the end of the 1950s, its advertising did not concentrate on space heating appliances and its sales forecasts were very pessimistic about growth prospects in the domestic market.[71] Moreover, the most novel aspect of the SWGB's marketing strategy in the early 1960s was a decision to sell supplies of bottled gas to consumers beyond the reach of its mains system.[72] The motives for this included the desire to stem the loss of the Board's customers to electricity and also to compete more effectively in the industrial market.[73] Sales of gas cylinders turned out to be disappointing, but the interesting feature of the initiative is that it suggests an attempt to extend the geographical reach of the Board within the South West, in contrast to the efforts to boost sales to existing customers which were being undertaken by other Boards at this time.[74]

By the mid-1960s the South Western Board had become more aware of the opportunities for sales growth.[75] It was reported that 'during 1964 and 1965 the Board mounted a large and intensive sales effort to lift the sales of appliances to the levels of the increased sales being enjoyed by other Boards.[76] Sales and service were reorganised, and the Board set about creating mobile sales teams to sell heating and other domestic appliances.[77] Sales forecasts were now much more ambitious. By 1967 the SWGB was predicting that domestic sales in the region would grow by 10 per cent in 1967/68, rising to 17 per cent per annum by 1969/70.[78] These were unprecedented rates of expansion for the Board, and one of the highest forecasts in the industry, justified on the grounds that the South West had been a late starter on domestic sales growth and so had the opportunity for catching up.[79]

In fact, sales did grow quite rapidly, although by 1970, the Board had fallen some distance behind its target for domestic sales, having reached only 110 million therms compared to the level of 123 million therms forecast in 1967.[80] Its rate of growth in the domestic sector continued to be below that attained by the industry as a whole in the second half of the 1960s. The Board had lost some customers as a result of price increases in 1966 and 1968 and had probably been too optimistic about the levels of consumption per domestic consumer which could be achieved.[81]

Underlying this was the continuing problem of the need to contain costs. The sales drive which began in the South West around 1963 does not seem to have been sustained for long. Advertising expenditure by the SWGB did not grow any faster than the national trend for the industry as a whole. The number of showroom and district sales staff in the South West grew from 311 in 1964 to 450 in 1965, as mobile sales teams were recruited but then fell back to 388 in 1966, hovering around 400 in the next two years.[82] Many other regions, including East Midlands, showed consistent growth in the number of sales staff during the 1960s.

The domestic market remained at the centre of the gas industry's attention until the late 1960s. The Boards hung onto industrial and commercial consumers as best they could in the face of strong competition from suppliers of oil and liquefied petroleum gas. With the discovery of North Sea gas, prospects for sales expansion opened up in the industrial market. The Gas Council and the Area Boards began to plan their expansion in this market.[83] Because of their respective geographical positions, the East Midlands was at the forefront of these developments while the South West was some way behind, but both Boards were beginning to experience a sharp upturn in industrial sales by the late 1960s. With a buoyant domestic market and excellent prospects in the industrial market, the kind of problems which the Boards had faced in the 1950s were at an end.

In assessing the sales records of the two Boards over the first twenty years of public ownership, it might be argued that the success of the East Midlands was due simply to its more favourable environment. Certainly the SWGB faced some formidable disadvantages. The price of gas in the South West was very high and this was bound to have had a detrimental effect on gas sales. The data in Table 3.10 reveal that, in the early 1960s, only the Scottish Board's prices were higher, at consumption levels of both 80 therms and 160 therms, than the SWGB. However, the table also shows that electricity in the South West was more expensive than in many other regions. The net effect, then, was that the difference between the prices of electricity and gas in the South West was on the large side, but not beyond comparison with some other Boards, such as the Scottish, North Western, and North Eastern. The East Midlands Gas Board was in a better position to compete with electricity on price than its South Western counterpart but was not in a uniquely favourable position when compared with all other regions.

Moreover, the pattern of sales growth in the regions cannot be explained solely by reference to price. In the years after 1957, when growth began to accelerate, sales expanded most in the more southerly parts of the country, and these were also the areas where gas prices were highest.[84]

Income levels might also help to explain variations in sales growth. However, it was not the case that consumers in the South West were too poor to afford central heating and space heating. A Gas Council's survey in 1968 found that the proportion of households with any form of central heating in the South West was 20 per cent. This was higher than for seven of the other Boards. As with the sales figures, a north-south divide was apparent. The five regions in the south of England all had figures of 20 per cent or higher (the highest being 27 per cent),

Table 3.10 A comparison of the prices of gas and electricity in different regions, and at two consumption levels, 1961

	Gas, d	80 therms electricity, d	Differential, per cent	Gas, d	160 therms electricity, d	Differential per cent
Scottish	2,608	1,600	63.00	4,584	3,200	43.25
Northern	1,880	1,600	17.50	3,360	3,200	5.00
North Western	2,064	1,600	29.00	3,744	3,200	17.00
North Eastern	2,320	1,400	65.71	3,648	2,800	30.29
East Midlands	1,856	1,600	16.00	3,248	3,200	1.50
West Midlands	1,744	1,600	9.00	3,104	3,200	−3.00
Wales	1,780	1,600	11.25	2,780	3,200	−13.13
Eastern	1,960	2,000	−2.00	3,920	4,000	−2.00
North Thames	2,068	2,000	3.40	4,136	4,000	3.40
South Eastern	1,920	1,920	0.00	3,840	3,840	0.00
Southern	2,080	1,800	15.56	4,160	3,600	15.56
South Western	2,480	1,800	37.78	4,400	3,600	22.22

while the seven Area Boards in the north and midlands were all below 20 per cent. The proportion for East Midlands was 18 per cent.[85] Thus the SWGB was in quite a favourable position with regard to the willingness of consumers to purchase central heating. Unfortunately, the share of gas in the central heating market was quite low in the South West, with consumers showing a preference for solid fuel and for oil. In contrast, the East Midlands Gas Board had managed to capture a higher share of the central heating market than any other Board.

The fact that demand first grew in the south of the country also leads us to downplay the significance of temperature as an explanatory variable. The demand for heating was assessed on the basis of 'degree days'. These essentially measure the extent and duration of the drop in temperature below some base level. Results on this measure for the twenty year period 1957 to 1977 reveal that the most southerly parts of the South West such as Cornwall recorded few degree days (i.e. were less cold) but the remainder of the SWGB area, including populous areas such as Bristol, Gloucester and Swindon differed little from the rest of the south of England.[86]

So, there were underlying differences between the regions, of which price was the most important, and income levels and temperature of much less significance but, on balance, these variables do not offer a full explanation of the poor performance of the South West in domestic space heating. Furthermore, we can point to some serious flaws in the marketing strategy of the South Western Board which help to build a richer and fuller picture of its relatively weak results.

A study by the management consultants, McKinsey, examined the relative strengths of the boards' marketing in the late 1960s. The East Midlands was found to have ample sales staff, and was well-focused on the central heating market. A higher proportion of its advertising was spent on central heating than for any other Board, and in absolute terms it spent the highest amount per consumer on advertising central heating. Its area of weakness was in turning leads into sales, possibly because of low commission rates for central heating sales, or because sales staff spent too high a percentage of their time on non-sales activities. The South West was shown to be short of selling manpower, and not carefully focused on central heating. Only 20 per cent of its planned advertising for 1968/69 was on central heating, compared to 64 per cent for East Midlands (although only two other Boards were above 25 per cent), and few of its showrooms had permanent central heating displays.[87]

There is also evidence of variation in the use of market research by regions. Market research was not much used by the South West until quite late in the period, while the East Midlands was one of the pioneers of the use of such techniques in the gas industry. In part this might be accounted for by the relative size of the two Boards. It tended to be the larger Boards such as North Western, North Thames, and East Midlands which established their own market research departments in the 1950s. But there may also have been differences of opinion about the usefulness of market research. It was said that the senior officers of the South Western Board did not believe that market research would tell them anything they didn't already know.[88] One consequence of this was that the SWGB was slow to realise that the image of its product among consumers was unfavourable compared to electricity.

6 Conclusion

The objective of this research has been to throw some new light on the long-running debate about the performance of the nationalised sector. As noted in the introduction, discussion about state-owned enterprise has been dominated by the question of government/industry relations and, in particular, the difficulty of reconciling the need for long-run strategic planning with the politicians' alleged proneness to short-term intervention.

While acknowledging that it is necessary to be cautious in generalising from a study of the experience of two regions within a single industry, the evidence presented here suggests that the significance of this issue can easily be exaggerated.[89] It seems plain that the Area Gas Boards were able to develop and implement their own long-term strategies with little direct intervention from Whitehall. These strategies were shaped mainly by geographic and economic conditions within the regions, rather than by government policy.

The South West was sparsely populated, and many potential customers were beyond the reach of a gas mains. It was far from the regions of the country where gas coal was mined and therefore incurred substantial transport costs in obtaining supplies of coal. It also lacked any alternative feedstocks during the 1950s. These factors drove up the South Western Board's costs compared to the industry average and meant that a strategy of retrenchment and the firm control of costs was appropriate for the Board. The East Midlands Board, on the other hand, enjoyed the advantage of access to cheap supplies of coke oven gas in the 1950s, and early access to North Sea gas in the 1960s. These favourable conditions made it easier for the Board to be competitive and to implement a sales drive from the late 1950s onwards.

The Boards made some strategic mistakes. The production strategy adopted by the South Western Board contributed significantly to its own problems. Given the high cost of producing gas from coal in the South West, and its lack of alternatives such as coke oven gas and imported methane, one might have expected the Board to have moved quickly into the production of gas from oil. But instead, the South Western Board locked itself into an expensive long-term coal contract in 1959, which added a premium to its already high costs throughout the 1960s. The reason for this decision was essentially that the Board sacrificed long-run advantage for some short-term cost benefits against a background of persistent deficits.

On the marketing side, the SWGB was very slow to appreciate the new opportunities which were opening up in the late 1950s in the domestic market for space heating. Unlike the East Midlands, it did not attempt a sales drive at that time. Some of its later marketing initiatives, such as the decision to sell bottled gas in rural areas were also not successful. The Board's forecasting was poor, and it was a latecomer in the field of market research. The unfavourable image of the gas industry in the South West, which must have contributed to a poor sales record, was also not addressed effectively.

The East Midlands Board also made some errors. In particular, its production strategy was not always compatible with its desire to increase sales. Because of the problems of coping with peak demand in the abnormally cold winter of 1962/63, the EMGB curtailed its sales drive on space heating for several years, switching its sales force towards the market for cookers and reducing their incentives. The Board also took the decision that it would aim to put sufficient capacity in place to meet future winters of such severity, in contrast to most other Boards. This decision meant that it had to tread carefully in promoting gas heating and its sales drive lost momentum for a number of years. There was, then, in the late 1960s, a lack of consistency between its production strategy and the aim of its marketing strategy of promoting and selling gas central heating.

The broader implications of these findings are that a range of geographic and economic factors beyond the control of the Area Boards must provide the major part of any explanation of performance variations within the gas industry although management were also important through their control of marketing and production strategies.

This is not to suggest that the Area Boards were unaffected either by economic policy in general or by policy initiatives aimed specifically at the nationalised sector. For example, the gas industry was severely hampered by the allocation of resources by central government in the first five years or so of public ownership. Area Boards were allocated far less steel and other materials than they would ideally have liked in the period up to 1953. This slowed down the Area Boards' plans for new gas works and the rebuilding of existing works. Marketing activities were constrained by the lack of capacity to meet peak loads. However, these shortages were probably unavoidable in the late 1940s and early 1950s as the economy recovered from the impact of the Second World War. Over the period 1950 to 1970 as a whole the Area Boards were provided with adequate funds for new investment. They were able to undertake a major programme of works reconstruction and integration during the 1950s. The transition to oil-based technology in the 1960s was, for most Area Boards, very rapid, while the subsequent shift into North Sea gas seems to have received generous funding from government.[90] The appraisal and control of investment also improved during the 1960s, largely due to pressure from the Treasury.[91] However, the Boards were able to make their own choices of new technology and do not seem to have been hampered by the 'technological nationalism' of politicians.

The actual role of government was well summarised by the Select Committee on Nationalised Industries:

> Broadly, apart from the appointment of Board members and a marginal interest in research and development and training and education, active Ministerial control has been predominantly concerned with financial and economic matters, especially investment programmes, prices, financial objectives, and surpluses, deficits and subsidies. But, as one academic witness emphasised, these do not touch on a great many factors which bear on the efficiency of the industries. Such matters as commercial policies and marketing machinery, personnel policies, labour relations, recruitment and promotion methods and internal organization have usually been regarded as lying within the industries' own sphere of decision. Furthermore, the Committee have received surprisingly little evidence that even the quality of services and consumer relations – matters in which Ministers might have been expected to take a great interest because of their political and public sensitivity – are the subject of Ministerial intervention, except when Ministers are pressured by parliamentary questions. Not surprisingly, though not necessarily correctly, the concern of Ministers has been almost exclusively confined to those matters in which money is directly involved.[92]

The influence of government policy was confined to certain, mainly financial, topics and the evidence from the gas industry does not support the view that the results of these policies in this period were particularly damaging. This is in line with the findings of Pryke's first book on the nationalised industries, which also looked at the 1950s and 1960s, although there is, perhaps, less evidence of government helping to raise performance than Pryke believed.[93] In practice, the Area Gas Boards retained autonomy in many important aspects of strategic decision-making and it is therefore vital to pay attention to the circumstances and experience of each region if an accurate picture of the history of the nationalised gas industry is to be built up.

Notes

1 I am grateful to Alan Booth and Joseph Melling for excellent supervision of the University of Exeter Ph.D. thesis upon which this article is based. John Wilson and two anonymous referees provided helpful comments on an earlier version of this paper. I accept full responsibility for the views expressed here.

2 *Select Committee on Nationalised Industries, Ministerial Control of the Nationalised Industries*

3 National Economic Development Office, *A Study of UK Nationalised Industries* (London: HMSO, 1976), pp. 8–9.

4 *Ibid.*, p. 35.

5 Richard Pryke, *Public Enterprise in Practice* (London: MacGibbon and Kee, 1971), pp. 448–456.

6 Richard Pryke, *The Nationalised Industries: Policies and Performance since 1968* (Oxford: Martin Robertson, 1981), p. 257.

7 *Ibid.*, pp. 259–264.

8 See John Vickers and George Yarrow, *Privatization: An Economic Analysis* (Cambridge, MA: MIT Press, 1988), pp. 9–39 for a careful discussion of these arguments.

9 General surveys of the history of the nationalised industries include William Ashworth, *The State in Business 1945 to the mid 1980s* (London: Macmillan, 1991); Terry Gourvish, 'The Rise (and Fall?) of State-Owned Enterprise' in Terry Gourvish and Alan O'Day (eds), *Britain since 1945* (London: Macmillan, 1991); Leslie Hannah, 'The Economic Consequences of the State Ownership of Industry, 1945–1990', in Roderick Floud and Donald McCloskey (eds), *The Economic History of Britain since 1700*, Volume 3 (Cambridge: Cambridge University Press, 1994). Historical studies of particular industries include William Ashworth, *The History of the British Coal Industry, Vol. 5, 1946–1982: The Nationalised Industry* (Oxford: Oxford University Press, 1986); T. R. Gourvish, *British Railways, 1948–1973* (Cambridge: Cambridge University Press, 1986); Leslie Hannah, *Engineers, Managers and Politicians: The First Fifteen Years of Nationalised Electricity Supply in Britain* (London: Macmillan, 1982).

10 Robert Millward, 'Productivity in the UK Services Sector: Historical Trends 1856–1985 and Comparisons with the USA 1950–85', *Oxford Bulletin of Economics and Statistics*, 52/4 (1990).

11 See Ashworth, *State in Business*, Ch 5 for an industry-by-industry survey.

12 Hannah, *Engineers, Managers and Politicians*, Ch. 14; Ashworth, *British Coal Industry*, pp. 659–662.

13 Hannah, 'Economic Consequences of the State Ownership of Industry, pp. 186–7; Ashworth, *State in Business*, pp. 86–7.

14 Ashworth, *State in Business*, pp. 178–85.

15 The standard history, which includes coverage of the nationalised era, is Trevor I. Williams, *A History of the British Gas Industry* (Oxford: Oxford University Press, 1981); a study of one of the Area Gas Boards has also been published, Malcolm Falkus, *Always Under Pressure: A History of North Thames Gas since 1949* (Basingstoke: Macmillan, 1988). For analysis of the reasons for nationalisation in the case of gas, see John F. Wilson, 'The Motives for Gas Nationalisation: Practicality or Ideology?' in Robert Millward and John Singleton (eds), *The Political Economy of Nationalisation 1920–1950* (Cambridge: Cambridge University Press, 1995).

16 Gas Act (1948), Section 1.

17 *Ibid.*, Section 41(1).

18 South Western Gas Board (hereafter SWGB) Annual Report, 1948/50, p. 2.

19 Gas Council Annual Report, 1948/50, Area Board Statistics.

20 Heyworth Report, pp. 17–9.

21 Gas Council Annual Report, 1959/60, pp. 168–9.
22 See Pryke, *Public Enterprise in Practice*, pp. 363–72, for a discussion of the gains from integration in the industry as a whole.
23 Pryke, *Public Enterprise in Practice*, pp. 371–2.
24 Williams, *History of the British Gas Industry*, pp. 143–7; H. Rush, 'The Broad Base of Technical Change in the Gas Industry', in K. Pavitt, *Technical Innovation and British Economic Performance* (London: Macmillan, 1980), p. 270.
25 Williams, *History of the British Gas Industry*, pp. 124–5.
26 C. Harlow, *Innovation and Productivity under Nationalisation* (London: George Allen and Unwin, 1977), pp. 157–160, 166–171; Williams, *History of the British Gas Industry*, pp. 126–8.
27 C. Harlow, *Innovation and Productivity under Nationalisation*, p. 168.
28 A. G. Jenkins, *The British Gas Industry, 1949 to 1970* (unpublished University of Exeter Ph.D. Thesis, 1998) pp. 172–5.
29 SWGB Conference of Head Office Staff, Aug 1959. Chairman's Committee Reports. National Gas Archive (hereafter NGA) BG31/SWO/CC/AM21/8.
30 C. H. Chester to R. H. Thomas, NCB Director General of Marketing, Aug 27th 1959. NGA Microfilm 590.
31 C. H. Chester to E. Flaxman, Commercial Assistant, British Railways West, Paddington Station, Aug 27th 1959. NGA Microfilm 590.
32 SWGB Chairman's Committee, Sept 1959, Minute 65. NGA BG31/SWO/CC/AM11.
33 Gas Council Annual Reports, 1958/59 pp. 147, 207; 1959/60, pp. 117, 175. The tonnage of coal used fell from 1.209 million tons in 1958/59 to 1.176 million tons in 1959/60.
34 C. H. Chester (SWGB) to Sir Henry Jones (Gas Council), NGA Microfilm 590.
35 SWGB Reference to the NBPI, Nov 1965, NGA Microfilm 87; NBPI Gas Price Reference, paper by Merrett Cyriax Associates/Chorley, Nov 1965, pp. 31–2, NGA Microfilm 89.
36 SWGB Chairman's Committee, March 1962, Minute 175, NGA BG31/SWO/CC/AM12. SWGB, 'Proposal for the Installation of Reforming Plants', Feb 1962, p. 1, NGA Microfilm 161.
37 Gas Council Annual Report, 1969/70, p. 10.
38 SWGB, 'Report on the Proposed Adoption of Steam Reforming Plants', Sept 1962, p. 92. NGA Microfilm 161.
39 SWGB Chairman's Committee, Dec 1962, Minute 127, NGA BG31/SWO/CC/AM13. SWGB Board Minutes, Feb 1st 1963, Minute 202, NGA BG31/SWO/MB/AM9.
40 SWGB Board Minutes: January 1966, Minute 196; April 1966, Minute 4; May 1966, Minute 36, NGA BG31/SWO/MB/AM10. SWGB Chairman's Committee Minutes: January 1966, Minute 172, NGA BG31/SWO/CC/AM14; Nov 1968, Minute 237, NGA BG31/SWO/CC/AM15.
41 SWGB Annual Report, 1966/67, p. 1.
42 Calculated from Gas Council Annual Reports, 1950/51 and 1957/58.
43 Figures in Gas Council Annual Reports show that supplies of coke oven gas were 172 million therms in 1964/65, 160 million therms by 1967/68 and 139 million therms by 1969/70.
44 Gas Council Annual Reports, 1964/65 and 1969/70.

45 East Midlands Gas Board (hereafter EMGB) Board Minutes, Nov 22nd 1960, p. 446, Minute 2657. NGA BG34/EMO/MB/AM14.
46 EMGB Board Minutes, Dec 1961, Appendix VIII, p. 474. Report on Gas Council meeting. NGA BG34/EMO/MB/AM15.
47 EMGB Board Minutes, May 1962, Appendix IV, pp. 192–4, NGA BG34/EMO/MB/AM16; EMGB Board Minutes, July 1963, Appendix VI, p. 353. NGA BG34/EMO/MB/AM17; EMGB Annual Report, 1964/65.
48 EMGB Annual Report, 1966/67, p. 5.
49 Gas Council Annual Report, 1965/66, pp. 8–9.
50 EMGB Annual Report, 1967/68, p. 5.
51 EMGB Board Minutes, July 1966, Appendix V, Report on Conversion of East Midlands to Natural Gas Supplies, NGA BG34/EMO/MB/AM21.
52 *Ibid.*, p. 3.
53 EMGB Annual Report, 1969/70, pp. 1–2, 13.
54 Falkus, *Always Under Pressure*, pp. 45, 48–50.
55 Jenkins, *British Gas Industry, 1949 to 1970*, pp. 206–12.
56 H. Jones, 'Future Development of the Gas Industry', Gas Council Commercial Policy Committee Memo CP2, Jan 1953, p. 3. NGA BG15/BG/CMK/AM1.
57 L. W. Andrew, 'Increasing the Domestic Load', *Gas World*, June 10th 1961, p. 869.
58 Falkus, *Always Under Pressure*, pp. 82–3; K Hutchison, *High Speed Gas* (London: Duckworth, 1987), pp. 214–18.
59 *Gas World*, Nov 2nd 1957, p. 823.
60 East Midlands advertising poster, NGA Microfilm 583.
61 *Gas Times*, July 1960, p. 22.
62 EMGB Annual Report, 1959/60, p. 11; EMGB Board Minutes, July 1959, p. 417, Proposals for the Establishment of Special Salesmen. NGA BG34/EMO/MB/AM13.
63 EMGB, 'The Consumption Characteristics of Domestic Users of Gas Space Heaters' (1962), Chapters II, VII. NGA Microfilm 757.
64 EMGB Board Minutes, Jan 1962, Appendix II, p. 504. Chief Engineer's Report. NGA BG34/EMO/MB/AM15.
65 EMGB Board Minutes, Jan 1962, Appendix III, p. 506. Commercial Manager's Report; EMGB Board Minutes, Jan 1962, p. 495, Minute 2940. NGA BG34/EMO/MB/AM15.
66 EMGB Board Minutes, Feb 1964, p. 199: Commercial Manager's Report on 1964/65 Publicity Budget, NGA BG34/EMO/MB/AM18; EMGB Board Minutes, June 1964, Minute 3532, NGA BG34/EMO/MB/AM19; EMGB meeting with Gas Council, Sept 29th 1966, NGA Microfilm 507.
67 SWGB Annual Reports, 1957/58 and 1958/59.
68 SWGB Chairman's Committee, Oct. 1960, Minute 62. NGA BG31/SWO/CC/AM12.
69 SWGB Chairman's Committee, Sept 1959, Minute 65; Nov 1959, Minute 90; NGA BG31/SWO/CC/AM11; July 1961, Minute 53, NGA BG31/SWO/CC/AM12; SWGB Chairman's Committee Reports, Aug 1959, Conference of Head Office Senior Staff, p. 2, NGA BG31/SWO/CC/AM21/8.
70 Area Development Manager's Letter and Report on Sales Development, SWGB Chairman's Committee Reports, May 1959, NGA BG31/SWO/CC/AM21/5.

71 For advertising strategy see SWGB Annual Report, 1958/59, p. 29; and for sales forecasts, SWGB Chairman's Committee Reports, Oct. 1958, NGA BG31/SWO/CC/AM20; SWGB Deputy Chairman's Committee, Feb 1959, NGA BG31/SWO/CC/AM19; SWGB Chairman's Committee Reports, March 1963, NGA BG31/SWO/CC/AM25/3. Further discussion of this evidence is in Jenkins, *British Gas Industry, 1949 to 1970*, pp. 226–7.

72 *Gas World*, 13 Jan 1962, p. 96.

73 Gas Council, 'Sales of LPG in Rural Areas', pp. 1–3, Gas Council Commercial Policy Committee, Memo CP 593, Jan 1963, NGA Microfilm 698; SWGB Chairman's Committee, Nov 1960, Minute 71, April 1961, Minute 11(g), NGA BG31/SWO/CC/AM12.

74 SWGB Annual Reports: 1964/65, p. 11; 1965/66, p. 15; SWGB Report of Commercial Manager to Chairman's Committee, April 1968, NGA BG31/SWO/CC/AM30/4; SWGB Chairman's Committee, Oct. 1960, Report on LPG, NGA BG31/SWO/CC/AM22/9.

75 SWGB meeting with Ministry of Power to discuss 1964 Capital Development Programme, May 4th 1964, p. 1. NGA Microfilm 87.

76 SWGB Reference to the National Board for Prices and Incomes, Nov 1965, [Ref No. SWGB 4 p. 2]. NGA Microfilm 87.

77 SWGB Annual Reports: 1962/63, p. 4; 1963/64, p. 3; 1964/65, pp. 3, 9.

78 D. G. Blagbrough, SWGB, to R. G. Huxtable, Gas Council, 21 Nov 1967. NGA Microfilm 505.

79 SWGB meeting with Gas Council to discuss 1968 Capital Development Programme, 7 Dec 1967, p. 4. NGA Microfilm 505.

80 SWGB Annual Report, 1969/70, p. 10.

81 SWGB meeting with Gas Council to discuss 1968 Capital Development Programme, 19 April 1968, p. 8. NGA Microfilm 505.

82 Gas Council and SWGB Annual Reports.

83 Williams, *History of the British Gas Industry*, pp. 210–22.

84 For more details see Jenkins, *British Gas Industry, 1949 to 1970*, pp. 237–40.

85 Gas Council Commercial Policy Committee, Memo CP 1041(b), April 1968, p. 5. NGA Microfilm 701.

86 Department of Energy, *Degree Days* (London: HMSO, 1977) p. 16. This makes use of non-standard regions. The South Western region (Devon and Cornwall only) had an annual mean of 1,835 degree days over 1957 to 1977. The Severn Valley region (comprising, very roughly, the rest of the SWGB area), had 2,097 degree days; in comparison, Thames Valley had 2,030, South Eastern 2,261, Wales 2,067, and Southern 2,114; the EMGB area was covered by Midland at 2,336 and East Pennines at 2,226.

87 McKinsey Reports for the Gas Council: 'Improving Marketing Operations in the Area Boards', Oct 1968, NGA BG15/BG/MCK/AX1; 'Mobilizing the Industry's Marketing Power', Oct 1968, NGA BG15/BG/MCK/AX2.

88 This attitude to market research amongst the senior personnel was reported to me by members of the South Western Gas Historical Society when I gave a paper to them in 1997.

89 In explaining variations in the performance of the nationalised industries, other historians have placed a good deal of emphasis on the business environment in which the industries were operating and on the strengths

and weaknesses of management: see, for example, Gourvish, 'Rise and Fall of State-owned Enterprise', pp. 127–30; Ashworth *State in Business*, pp. 90–164, 189.

90 For discussion of the speed of the transition to North Sea gas see Williams, *History of the British Gas Industry*, pp. 189–90.

91 Pryke, *Public Enterprise in Practice*, pp. 339–46.

92 Select Committee on Nationalised Industries, Report on Ministerial Control of the Nationalised Industries, Vol. I, para 51.

93 Pryke, *Public Enterprise in Practice*.

4 Industrialisation, pollution and estuarine rescue*

John Hassan

1 Introduction

Contrary to some of the charges, implied or explicit, levelled against the discipline,[1] economic history, as E. L. Jones recognised some time ago,[2] is well equipped to shed light on the environmental consequences of industrialisation. This paper seeks to bring an economic-historical perspective on the causes and effects of environmental pollution. For the purposes of exposition, the processes involved are conceptualized in terms of a four-stage scheme, framed with reference to the impacts upon the water cycle in England since the industrial revolution.

One aim is to capture one of the principal impacts of industrialisation, namely the generation of wastes on such a scale that the assimilative capacity of the environment was exceeded and serious pollution resulted. Having established this principle in section 2, section 3 sets out the four-stage scheme more formally. A central feature of this is to conceive water and waste water as joint products. Yet another aim is to explain the tendency for pollution to be displaced across both space and time as a prominent characteristic of modern environmental history. These issues are related in section 4 to the history of water pollution in England since the industrial revolution, and are illustrated by reference, in particular, to the experience of two of England's greatest estuaries, the Mersey and the Tyne.

2 Pressure on the natural environment

As proven, economic reserves of resources like fossil fuel have tended to increase by considerably more than the rate at which they were used, the risk that they will eventually become exhausted is not the immediate threat posed to society by the resource-intensive growth initiated by the industrial revolution. The principal challenge has been

DOI: 10.4324/9781003331506-4

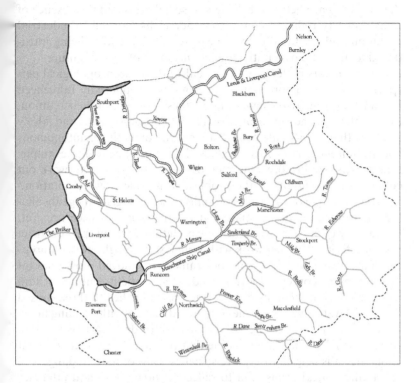

from the effects of the production of unprecedented volumes of waste matter which proceeded in tandem with the increased output of goods. This led to major environmental, and arguably, socio-economic, disturbances. To describe the erosion of the ability of the air and water environments to perform ecological and economic functions vital to humanity as 'market failure' hardly describes the seriousness of this development. For example, the permanent, conceivably catastrophic, changes in climate some believe the world is beginning now to experience can be explained by alterations in the chemistry of the atmosphere caused by the discharge of 'greenhouse gases', a process that was started by the industrial revolution.[3]

Scholars from many disciplines, including social and environmental historians such as Hamlin, Sheail and Luckin, have contextualised the environmental problems that have occurred over the last two centuries.[4] Often sympathetically they have described how individuals, institutions and society have developed adaptive strategies to the environmental conflicts that accompanied industrialisation. A series of more economic-historical accounts, such as Dingle's, have suggested that a divergence between private and social costs and the absence of clear property rights to common resources like air led to industrial pollution and, eventually, to a measure of intervention being introduced to at least partly mitigate such instances of market failure.[5]

Other scholars preferring a more cultural and anthropological perspective, are less impressed by explanations supposedly influenced by Hardin's tragedy-of-the-commons thesis[6] which, in their opinion, overemphasizes the significance of deficient property rights and falsely assumes that individuals behave as selfish, competitive, autonomous beings, untouched by social values. It would appear, for example, that groups like inshore fishermen do have the capacity to work out collaborative solutions to the problem of marine over-exploitation.[7] Douglas' critique of the way economists and ecologists allegedly analyse environmental disturbances barely falls short of caricature. Yet, the validity of perspectives that view pollution as a cultural construct may be admitted.[8] In her work with Wildavsky, Douglas raised important questions about how societies rank risk.[9] Indeed most relevant in the present context is *why* should late-twentieth century Britain invest billions in virtually eliminating the public health threat posed by coastal waters while, on the other hand and notwithstanding much hand-wringing, it seems prepared to live with a daily carnage on dangerous roads? These authors argue that to understand such apparent anomalies it is helpful to explore societies' view of natural dangers in moral and ethical terms, and to reflect on how power and influence are distributed especially between 'border' or peripheral phenomena such as environmental pressure groups and the centre, including the government.

Attempts to work out administrative and political solutions in the past to the problems of air and water pollution may have displayed ingenuity. However, the resource- and waste-intensive growth inaugurated by the industrial revolution was on such a scale that attempts to curtail pollution might eventually be nullified, if only because of the advent of geometric growth rates in economic and demographic activity. Further, the difficulty of securing enduring, long-term solutions to environmental damage arose less from ill-defined property rights *per se*, as from the easy access by *many* sectors with conflicting claims on air and water resources. Also fundamental was the liability of pollution to accumulate over time, both physically and also in terms of the financial and other costs it bequeathed to later generations. For example, for a while the emission into the environment of small amounts of stock pollutants, such as cadmium, mercury, lead and polychlorinated biphenyl (PCB) seemed to impose negligible costs on society. However, over time the failure to constrain the growth of emissions would represent, from an *ex post* perspective, a considerable threat due to the build-up of the pollutants beyond a particular threshold when they became a grave risk to human health.[10] Not dissimilar processes of inter-generational pollution transfer have manifested themselves recently as ozone depletion, acidification and global warming, the build-up of the polluting gases having started decades earlier. Because CO_2, N_2O and chlorofluorocarbons have atmospheric lifetimes of well over a century, their discharge into the environment produces a long-term, irreversible stock of pollutants beyond our control.[11] In less dramatic ways resort to cheap or inadequate methods of waste disposal had the effect of bequeathing a huge debt to late-twentieth century society, as will be seen below.

When confronted with matter out of place cultural values condition responses. The emergence of pollution may also be described in functional terms. Gross pollution occurs when natural eco-systems are so overloaded with waste matter that the normal processes of dilution and purification cannot be performed. It was not just that the presence of human or trade wastes in a river constituted an aesthetic affront: while it could absorb a certain amount of foreign matter and break it down into harmless substances, such as phosphates and nitrates, the river having used up much of its oxygen in this process eventually may lose its capacity for self-purification. The water becomes anaerobic and septic, organic waste is reduced to a different, harmful set of end-products, and putrefaction occurs.[12] During the twentieth century the assimilative capacity of many English estuaries was overwhelmed, levels of dissolved oxygen fell to zero and aquatic life was extinguished.

Pollution was not an invention of the industrial revolution, the desertification of the fertile crescent and thirteenth-century London smog being but two examples that predated it. But the industrial revolution did much more than 'explode the scale' of this process, as Jones put it.[13] The technological innovations associated with early industrialisation led to the fossil fuel inheritance, created by solar energy and geological forces over hundreds of millions of years, being unlocked and eagerly exploited. This allowed society to move into a state of energy abundance, energy consumption in Britain, for example, increasing by a factor of sixty between 1700 and 1900.[14] Displaying some comparisons with these trends were the organisational and technological improvements which allowed water undertakers to tap distant catchments, outside the natural gathering grounds of the towns they supplied. This enabled water use per head in several British cities to increase by a factor of about five in the century after 1850.[15]

Thus society became very much more energy- and water-intensive than it had been. Although there were considerable historical variations in energy-economy relationships, very broadly energy utilisation increased in the early stages of industrialisation with the growth of smokestack industries, before eventually declining as services and consumer goods assumed greater importance much later. Plotting energy consumption per head against gross domestic product per head in the UK from 1830 to 1955 shows that the energy-intensity of output grew rapidly in the early stages of industrialisation before eventually subsiding.[16] Similar data on water consumption has not to my knowledge been collated; such a task would be extremely difficult given the fragmentary and inconsistent nature of nineteenth-century evidence. However, it is probable that water use per head followed not an altogether different trajectory, judging from consumption patterns of countries at different stages of development. In the 1910s in Indian cities where wells were mainly relied on water consumption per head was about 8–10 gallons per head per day (ghd), compared to typical figures in France of 40–60 ghd, while in American cities consumption had risen to 50–90 ghd.[17]

No doubt the burning of fossil fuels and the exploitation of distant catchments sustained economic growth and brought great improvements in domestic comfort. In this connection much of the coal burned and about two-thirds of the water supplied to many nineteenth-century cities were used within the home. However, the improved delivery of fuel and water occurred step-by-step with an expanding output of polluting waste matter. Coal, responsible for ninety-five per cent of Western Europe's primary energy sources by the 1920s, was a dirtier source of energy than those it typically replaced. In the process of combustion coal emits much carbon dioxide, water vapour, unburned hydrocarbons, soot, dust and smaller quantities of waste gases and especially sulphur dioxide. Similarly, the act of water consumption may yield utility, but it is invariably followed by the discharge of dirty effluent into the environment.

Furthermore, nineteenth century urbanisation and industrialisation also led to heavier concentrations of populations and economic activity, or 'species packing'. The effects of the discharge of exceptional quantities of waste matter into rather confined environments, and the collapse of the normal scavenging functions of air and water, are implied rather than proved by the kind of evidence available to the nineteenth-century historian.

Contemporaries, though, had little doubt that the discharges from coal fires and engines caused the sooty rain, the discoloured, blackened buildings and various, non-specific symptoms of ill-health such as 'nausea, vomiting, bronchial and respiratory complaints ... and a general feeling of malaise'.[18] In particular it was felt that these emissions contributed to the dirty pall and smoggy conditions that hung over the late Victorian city. Contemporary records indicate that cities like London and Manchester became evermore foggy from roughly the late eighteenth century to the late nineteenth or early twentieth centuries.[19] Evidence of declining water quality also tends to be indirect. Rivers were so contaminated that people falling into them risked death by poisoning rather than drowning, they turned black with pollution and fish catches plummeted.

The above may be a simplistic account which ignores many variations and subtleties within the general picture. For example, that fuel and water are different categories of natural resources has been overlooked, with focus being placed on the similar functions of the hydrosphere and atmosphere as 'waste receptors'; any attempt to underline the conflict-ridden nature of energy-intensive growth by reference to the second law of thermodynamics, which implies that economic activity progressively transforms useful resources into less useful matter, such as heat, has been abandoned as irrelevant to the main argument;[20] and references to pollution transfers from one medium to another, particularly from energy-consuming activities to the water environment, have been omitted as an unnecessary, if quite important, complication. It is felt that the main trends are so emphatic that such subtleties can be ignored.

Since the early nineteenth century numerous efforts have been made to combat pollution through technical improvements and legislative reforms. To summarise a very considerable literature, however, large sectors remained unregulated and the discharge of untreated, polluting emissions continued unabated into the second half of the twentieth century. For example, the coal smoke issuing from the entire domestic sector and the raw household and trade effluent discharged by the population living near coasts or estuaries, not less than thirty per cent of the total, lay outside useful control until after 1950. The progress made to control other sources of air and water pollution was slow and uneven. For much of the period covered by this paper the actual penalties or other disincentive imposed on polluting firms and individuals were often so weak or avoidable as to impose a negligible cost on polluters.

3 A four-stage scheme

The foregoing may now be condensed into a scheme which describes the environmental problems created by expanding water use in Britain since the industrial revolution as a four-stage process. Briefly, *firstly* water and waste water are conceived as joint products, the output of which rose alongside that of the economy; *secondly* assimilative capacity of the environment was overwhelmed; *thirdly*, various factors made effective policy responses difficult to conceive. *Finally*, programmes were eventually developed to rescue an appallingly degraded water environment.

To elaborate on these stages, *firstly* it is realistic to conceptualize water and waste water as joint products because the act of consumption was invariably followed by the discharge of effluent, the two acts sometimes coinciding as in the flushing of sewers and water closets. Furthermore, the water suppliers have generally also managed sewerage, virtually all household waste water and even much industrial effluent ultimately passing through the water industry's sewage treatment works (STWs). The charges imposed on the users of these facilities in the nineteenth century were minimal, sewerage rates, for example, were heavily subsidized and certainly took no account of external costs.

Secondly, the growth of waste emissions in due course overwhelmed the assimilative capacity of rivers and pollution ensued. This can be viewed as the result of the extremely undeveloped state of the markets for environmental quality in Victorian Britain and 'the absence of a price-induced market-clearing process'.[21] The argument can be set out formally as a set of equations. The exposition, which partially follows Pearce,[22] as usual in such instances is not intended to be tested against empirical data which, in any case, are unobtainable for most of the relevant parameters. Some may feel the exercise is superfluous, but it is retained to show the dynamic relationships between the production of goods, waste, assimilative capacity, and pollution, and the cumulative effects of 'rationale' behaviour.

Consider the production of water and waste water as the joint products of the water industry, where w denotes the clean water supplied by the industry to households or firms, and e refers to waste (effluent returned to the water cycle). The money wage is denoted by m and L is the quantity of labour input. Further, p denotes the price of an output, and in the case of the waste product free disposal implies $p_e = 0$. For the sake of simplicity assume a single non-labour input K, where the per unit cost of this input is denoted c. Production is characterized by a process of transformation of the non-labour input into useful clean water and dirty waste water. It follows, where the rate of profit is written r,

$$pw + p_e e = (cK + mL)(r + r) \tag{1}$$

Since the commodity *w* gives a positive utility it can command a positive price, hence $p_w > 0$. Waste water, *e*, yields disutility and cannot command a positive price. If, however, the water industry were required to internalize the wider costs involved in its disposal practices, these would enter as a further input and the above equation could be rewritten as:

$$p_w w = (cK + mL)(1 + r) - p_e e \qquad (2)$$

In such a situation the water industry would wish to reduce such costs, so as to produce purer, less polluting effluent. However, this does not describe histofrical reality. As explained above, little private expense or penalty was incurred in waste creation. Under these conditions the increased output of polluting waste would, therefore, be largely unrestrained.

As long as the flow of effluent does not exceed the assimilative capacity (termed *A*) of rivers pollution does not occur. Pollution (*P*) happens when water resources are so modified by effluent that their normal functions, such as sustaining fisheries and supplying drinking water, are undermined. Breaking down waste depletes oxygen levels, potentially undermining the river's capacity for self-purification. There is no pollution, that is $P_t = 0$, as long as $e_t \leq A_t$. However, the discharge of effluent, being largely unrestrained, will eventually lead to the point being reached where $P_{t+1} > 0$, that is where $e_{t+1} > A_{t+1}$, and assimilative capacity is seriously undermined (where $A_{t+2} < A_{t+1}$). Not only do increased emissions of waste contribute to the growth of pollution, but this is exacerbated by the effects of past pollution in reducing the river's assimilative capacity. Thus it follows,

$$P_{t+2} = e_{t+2} - A_{t+2} > e_{t+1} - A_{t+1} \qquad (3)$$

The moment described in equation (3) is when pollution starts to get worse. It may not, as yet, represent the gross pollution of waters involving serious contamination and the elimination of fish life. But the riparian environment often did suffer such corruption in twentieth century England.

In the *third* stage society begins to address the need to reverse these trends but extreme difficulty in accommodating the conflicting claims of water users is encountered. Despite widespread revulsion, the attempts to develop effective policy responses to the problem of river pollution were confounded by many difficulties, not least the public good, free rider and externality properties that distinguish environmental cleanliness, and also the multiple-use characteristics of water. Such problems are inherent in water use and are examples of market failure which are fully explored in modern economics, but which the Victorians had yet to conceptualise.

Cultural beliefs and unsoundly based bodies of knowledge also conditioned the way Victorians approached these problems. On the one hand faith was widespread in the capacity of the natural environment, especially of tidal waters and to a lesser extent of rivers, to absorb and purify pollution. Relic beliefs in the capaciousness, infinity and purgative powers of the sea in particular were barely dislodged by the march of technology and progress in the nineteenth century. The sea was 'cruel', unlimited and unknown felt Harry Jones in 1890.[23] Similar notions entertained by the Romantic poets, Ruskin and T. H. Huxley, while conveniently helping to legitimise the sea's employment as a global lavatory, survived alongside a fatalistic acceptance by many Victorians of *localised* symptoms of pollution as the inevitable and unavoidable price to be paid for industrial expansion.[24] As Herbert Philips said of smoke pollution: 'it requires that a nuisance shall be very serious before people will go out of their way to make a formal complaint, they generally grumble and do nothing'.[25]

Whether driven by economic or cultural forces delayed or inadequate responses to declining environmental quality led to pollutants accumulating in the environment so that pollution displacement, across time and space, became a characteristic feature of British environmental history in this period.

Fourthly and finally, rescue programmes were conceived especially during the second half of the twentieth century. Pearson having synthesised a great deal of modern empirical evidence, has theorised the factors that have influenced the supply and demand for environmental quality, and his account has some bearing on this discussion. Pearson indicates that testing of the so-called environmental Kuznets curve (EKC) hypothesis suggests that the demand for some forms of environmental quality rose as incomes grew; a deterioration in environmental quality appeared to be a temporary or natural progression in the early stages of development; subsequently preferences changed, conditioned by scientific, medical, educational and social advances which contributed to a better understanding of the impacts of pollution; further, higher incomes seemed to lead countries to regard environmental protection as more affordable, and they accordingly devoted more resources to securing higher environmental standards.[26]

Empirical testing reveals the EKC hypothesis to be more valid for localised, short-term forms of water and air pollution, similar to the kinds commented upon in this paper, rather than for more global, long-term, inter-generational pollution transfers that undermine the planet's resource stocks, such as its forests. My own account, nevertheless, does emphasize the tendency for past policy deficiencies to leave a legacy, both in the sense that a neglect of the water industry's physical assets means that the eventual cost of restoring this physical capital builds up over time, and in the form of an accumulation of contamination in the natural environment. It will shown below that many estuaries had become quite revolting, aesthetically and olfactory, by the 1960s and early 1970s. Their pollution seemed to have exceeded the limits of social acceptability.

In the following sections some considerations influencing society's decision to prioritize the eradication of estuarine filthiness will be explored. By the 1970s narrow, monetary estimations of the benefits accruing from environmental investment began to be supplemented by an acknowledgement of the value of amenity and aesthetic gains. Other factors that affected attitudes towards coastal conservation were higher incomes, changes in leisure patterns and a consumer rights dimension to environmental demands. Ultimately, the restoration of coastal waters to a pre-industrial purity became a national task, as confirmed in a series of decisions and statements made after 1997 by the deputy prime minister, John Prescott, and the environment minister, Michael Meacher.

4 Estuarine decline and recovery

The argument may now be illustrated by closer reference to the history of water pollution. The following account focuses on the experience of two of England's premier's estuaries, the Mersey and the Tyne. Nowhere were the deleterious effects of policy inadequacies more apparent than for estuarine waters. They did, of course, carry a heavy pollution load, especially when receiving effluent from heavily polluted rivers or canals. Rather than provide a detailed historical chronicle of the two estuaries, their fate will be set within the broader context of the history of sewage pollution and explored in terms of the four-stage sequence outlined above.

The English estuaries are a valuable resource. Estuarine sites offered many attractions for industry, including ease of effluent disposal, a means of cheap transport, and access to vast supplies of water for cooling and also, to some extent, steam-raising and process purposes. For the populations living near to these waters they provided an extremely cheap way of getting rid of untreated waste. This perceived 'privilege' was of great monetary value to coastal municipalities, leaving them with sewerage rates only some thirty-eight per cent of those charged in the larger inland towns.[27] English estuaries are also a significant ecological resource: the home of commercial fisheries and internationally important as nursery or over-wintering areas for numerous marine species. Shallow off-shore waters are also most important for marine life, including plankton, and contain the spawning grounds for many fish.

Some economic and physical differences between the Mersey and Tyne systems may be noted. The Mersey-Irwell system was one of the most densely populated and most intensively exploited catchments in the country. Almost as soon as streams left their headwaters they were seriously polluted, crude effluent emitted from mills and bleach works often being of better quality than the receiving waters. The Mersey not only took the water-borne wastes of Merseyside but also much of that from south-east Lancashire and north Cheshire (see map). By contrast, the Tyne drained a generally sparsely populated area. Even though serious pollutants were received from the North Pennines lead-mining industry, the river reached its tidal stretches in a comparatively good condition. The Tyne was England's premier salmon river.

4.1   The joint production of water and waste

Turning now to the four-stage chronology: a major reason for demographic and economic growth leading to water pollution was the progressive replacement from the early Victorian years of physical and other dry conservancy methods by the water-carriage system of domestic waste disposal. The change was vital: town waste disposal became an integral part of the water cycle. To improve the cleanliness of the home and residential districts steps were taken to introduce water closets and to drain houses into sewers. Indeed, from the 1840s it was customary for local legislation to require this.

With the gradual introduction of water closets and other water appliances water consumption grew rapidly in Victorian England. As elsewhere, the industrial and demographic expansion of Merseyside and Tyneside, the sewering of these conurbations and their conversion to water carriage, led to a great increase in water consumption and the discharge of effluent. This derived also from the success in exploiting extensive and remote catchments. Liverpool and Manchester had gone beyond local sources to tap the Pennine districts of Rivington and Longdendale in the 1850s. Later, they made the more fundamental move to develop extra-regional catchments, the Thirlmere project being authorized in 1879 and the Vyrnwy scheme coming on stream in

1891, while Catcleugh reservoir in the Cheviots was delivering water to Newcastle-upon-Tyne by 1907. By 1947 between sixty-five and seventy per cent of Liverpool's and Manchester's water came by aqueduct from central Wales and the Lake District, some thirty per cent from the Pennines, with only five per cent or less drawn from local rivers.[28] This made possible the huge increase in water consumption shown in Table 4.1.

The water supplied through the mains was used for many purposes. In Liverpool domestic consumption accounted for 58.5 per cent of total consumption in 1902, industry and trade took 29.6 per cent, while 'public' uses including street cleansing and sewer flushing absorbed 5.7 per cent.[29] Whatever the purpose, after use water became the 'liquid waste of the community',[30] all of which eventually made its way to the estuaries. The volume of raw domestic sewage discharged by Liverpool into the Mersey in 1927, 30 million gallons daily, was very similar to the current rate of water consumption.[31] All domestic effluent was discharged into the estuary, where it joined not only trade effluent discharged from shoreline chemical, petroleum and other processing industries, but also a significant pollution load carried by polluted streams from throughout the catchment with its population of 5 million. Most of the channels in the Mersey-Irwell basin were industrial rivers where, for example, seventy-five per cent of the dry weather flow consisted of effluent. But the pollution load entering the estuaries, especially the Mersey, was especially and unnaturally large, because of the heavy reliance of urban water supplies on extra-regional sources. By the early 1970s the Tyneside population, which approached one million, discharged some 910 cubic metres of raw sewage daily, and a range of engineering, chemical and other trade premises emptied 680 cubic metres of industrial effluent per day.[32]

Table 4.1 Estimates of total water consumption in three cities (millions of gallons per day)

Liverpool	Newcastle	Manchester
1846: 2.8	1831: 0.2	1829: 1.1
1882: 16.0	1870: 6.8	1857: 9.5
1902: 27.0	1911: 17.5	1882: 18.3
1938: 39.9	1931: 20.9	1938: 50.4
1948: 45.7s	1951: 29.8	1948: 62.5

Source: J. Hassan, *A history of water in modern England and Wales* (Manchester: Manchester University Press), p. 53.

4.2 Assimilative capacity exceeded

Much earlier the triumph of harnessing the resources of extensive gathering grounds had led to the assimilative capacity of small, industrial rivers like the Tame and Irwell being overwhelmed. Ill-equipped to receive unprecedented quantities of foul sewage, and with users able to externalise the social costs of their employment as public drains, they eventually became heavily polluted (see equations 1–3). Eventually, emitting the characteristic rotten egg smell of hydrogen sulphide associated with this condition, they became incapable of supporting life. The ecologies of even less threatened streams were affected, reflected in the catch of the six leading English salmon rivers falling from 185,000 per year in the 1870s to less than 50,000 per year by the 1940s.[33]

The biological and physical interactions contributing to the decline of rivers are extremely complex, but they can recuperate. During the winter thanks to increased flow induced by seasonal floods, tidal and other influences the level of dissolved oxygen in estuaries will recover from the summer 'sag'. It was indeed not for many years that the estuaries displayed the worst symptoms of environmental distress. Complaints about the Mersey's condition were voiced earlier than for the Tyne. In 1899 the Conservator of the Mersey Docks and Harbour Board (M.D.H.B.) complained of the severe pollution caused by fifty years of crude sewage being discharged from both shores of the estuary.[34] In the absence of long-term sets of consistent data one has to fall back upon fairly impressionistic evidence. This suggests that the most serious deterioration of the estuaries occurred comparatively recently, largely concentrated, in fact, in the period from the 1930s to the 1960s. This was when the Tees was exposed to the greatest pressure. Between 1931 and 1966 the weight of tar acids and cyanide and the total biochemical oxygen demand (BOD) of industrial effluent discharged into this estuary increased between two- and sixteen-fold.[35]

With respect to fisheries, a good guide to water quality, fishing boats regularly worked the Mersey estuary for shrimps, soles and whitings, forty vessels being active in 1910 and some still operating in the 1930s, before they virtually disappeared after the second world war.[36] The most graphic symptom of the Tyne's environmental deterioration was the collapse of salmon rod catches from 129,100 in 1870 to around 5,000 annually or less in the interwar period and to under 1,000 per annum in the 1950s. Netbuoy claimed: 'The loss of the Tyne is England's greatest single fishery disaster … Its magnitude in terms of food supply and economic wealth is difficult to measure, but staggering'.[37] The principal cause of the collapse, which also affected migratory trout, was the inability of the smolts to survive their journey from spawning grounds through the virtually poisonous mid-stretches of the estuary to the sea.

As previously indicated the BOD of effluent may so deplete oxygen levels that the channel becomes septic, putrefaction occurs and aquatic life becomes extinct. By 1927 for some miles along the Tyne below Newcastle the level of dissolved oxygen had fallen to zero.[38] By 1936 the river was nothing but an 'open sewer ... the concentration and semi-stagnation of polluting matter make the upper portion of the estuary virtually into a septic tank'.[39] The problem continued to grow incrementally partly because of increased discharges. Also, the slow flushing time of this and many other estuaries led to pollutants becoming attached to sedimented particles, which eventually settle on mud flats and salt marshes. Further, on the Tyne sludge solids, far from being scoured away by tidal action, were pushed back up the estuary by incoming tides to accumulate on the river bottoms.[40] By 1969 estuarine conditions may have reached their worst ever levels. A public inquiry taking place in Newcastle's Moot Hall had to be adjourned because of the stench from the river, reminiscent of an incident during London's 'Great Stink' over a century earlier.

Measures of dissolved oxygen levels were taken from the Mersey estuary in the 1930s and have been recorded regularly since the late 1960s. Taking all due care to allow for factors which might affect the significance of the readings, these clearly show that this was the period of the estuary's sharpest ecological decline.[41] The falling levels of dissolved oxygen in the 1950s and 1960s have been attributed to the 'dramatic industrial developments around the estuary', which took place during these years.[42] Devoid of oxygen in the summer months, the Mersey became an extremely offensive and smelly nuisance for the local population with many manifestations of gross pollution, the foul odour of hydrogen sulphide being noticeable in the upper reaches, and nearer the estuary's mouth '... lumps of crude sewage and balls of fat [were] deposited on the foreshore'.[43]

4.3 *Conflicts over use and pollution displacement*

There is now a large literature that touches on the history of water pollution. It tends to focus on the nineteenth century, with some papers extending into the interwar years. Hamlin has acknowledged the existence of a failure to solve the 'social problems of water supply, wastes disposal and river use' before 1914. This he attributed in particular to the rivalries and adversarial conflicts which so characterized the scientific and professional communities in these fields.[44] Elsewhere, however, he and other scholars anxious to set problems within their historical context and unwilling to be judgmental, have stressed the hugely complex problems of waste disposal facing the Victorians, the absence of an effective abatement technology for much of the period, and ratepayer resistance to costly public works. They are, therefore, willing to acknowledge the constructive efforts, even the 'extraordinary achievement', of municipal officers, civil servants, scientists and other professionals, in the manner they addressed the environmental challenges facing society.[45] With a longer time frame, however, one of the 'excuses' for Victorian difficulties, the absence of or bewilderment about suitable abatement techniques, becomes less relevant.

By the interwar period the scientific and engineering impediments to effective sewage treatment had been largely overcome.[46] It is certainly appropriate to go beyond suggestions of human or institutional failings in explanations for the long-term decline in the quality of English waters until the 1950s, and in some cases including tidal waters, until the 1980s, and search for more fundamental factors, such as economic influences. For example, crucially the potentially profitable and invariably cost-covering activity of water supply attracted a great deal more investment and (municipal and private) entrepreneurial attention than the loss-making business of sewage disposal. For most of the period water-supply schemes attracted much higher levels of capital spending than STWs, with the consequence that the large quantities of waste water returned to the hydrological system were of poor quality.[47]

Another challenge was the task of reconciling the divergent interests of water users. Even when much later in the 1970s schemes to rescue the Mersey were being planned, professionals were sceptical whether they could ever be realised. According to one observer there was 'an unwillingness to pay' the costs of meeting the 'insatiable demands for more and better [water] services ... The two are irreconcilable'.[48] Tidal waters, it has been said, 'have a number of functions which do not always go well together'.[49] The same is true of inland waters. Illustrative of the public good and free rider problems associated with environmental cleanliness, towns like Bury and Macclesfield were strongly disinclined to invest in STWs when the main beneficiaries were not rate-payers, but downstream users of a cleaner river who had made no contribution to this expenditure.[50] Occasionally the same authorities acted more constructively. This only underlines the confusion of policy objectives. Similarly, a major interest like the Lancashire textile manufacturers adopted contradictory positions on pollution control.

As a group they both craved some improvement in water quality within catchments, but more characteristically strenuously insisted on their perceived legal right, and the economic need, to pollute.[51] These problems were complicated by the lack of complete understanding over much of the period of such processes as water-borne infection, or the capacity of rivers to absorb and purify wastes. In such circumstances it is hardly surprising that there were delays in devising effective pollution abatement policies, and the instinct of the late Victorians was to 'throw away' the difficulty.[52]

Failure to devise better solutions at source led to the costs of pollution being shifted elsewhere. The completion of Bazalgette's great interceptor sewers in the mid-1860s and the building of downstream outfalls for the release of untreated sewage into the lower reaches of the Thames, led to the deterioration of hygienic conditions in estuarine towns like Barking.[53] Later, the actions of the Thames Conservancy in trying to protect the waters under its jurisdiction 'had merely removed the problem downstream' with, for example, bargemen now dumping their waste here rather than in the upper reaches.[54] In nineteenth-century Bristol the emptying of the city's raw household and trade sewage into stretches of urban river and harbour led to an accumulating problem of faecal contamination. Improvisations were resorted to, involving the dispatch of Bristol's foul waters into the Avon and thence, by tidal action, into the sea. The long-held vision of a trunk sewer to the coast was not realised, however, until the 1960s.[55]

Partly due to the flow of contamination along overloaded rivers, as well the effects of direct discharges of raw sewage into tidal waters, pollution, therefore, tended to shift towards the coasts. There was consternation when it became clear in the 1900s that the open waters around England had suffered this fate.[56] The reputation of several resorts was compromised due to the faecal contamination of beaches and many outbreaks of typhoid were traced back to the sewage pollution of inshore fisheries.

Committed to the 'dilute and disperse' principle as a cornerstone of its environmental policy, the government adopted a hands-off approach to the pollution of tidal waters, leaving local authorities with the responsibility for managing this problem until the 1970s.[57] As elsewhere conflicts of purpose among users of these resources paralysed policy locally. Various groups objected to the pollution of estuaries, including those representing navigation, fishery, public health and amenity interests. A crucial difficulty was that the agency which was expected to take the lead in coordinating waste management, namely local government, was also the major polluter. The coastal municipal authorities greatly valued the financial savings enjoyed by discharging sewage into tidal waters. As Liverpool Corporation claimed: 'Apart from the statutory right of the Corporation to discharge sewage into the Mersey estuary, sewage disposal by dilution, especially as applied to tidal waters, is universally recognised as a right and proper method of sewage disposal'.[58]

Earlier, before 1914, expressions of concern on Merseyside about the estuary's pollution were rather muted from fisheries and public health interests, other than during the shellfish contamination scare in the 1900s. On the contrary, city officers were proud of the achievements of flushing the streets and converting to the water-carriage system, which led to millions of gallons of foul sewage being discharged daily into the estuary. Even more directly over 60,000 tons of ash pit refuse was annually dumped directly into the sea by hopper barge.[59] The opposition to the resultant pollution of the estuary came principally from the M.D.H.B., concerned that the 'enormous increase in the amount of crude sewage and solid matter poured into the river' led to accumulations of deposits, silting and channel alterations.[60] Dredging, carried on continuously from 1890, removed over 6,000 tons of material per hour over the next four decades. The M.D.H.B. viewed with great anxiety moves by the local authorities to extend their boundaries with the intention of increasing their discharges of raw sewage, matters coming to a head in 1927, following steps by the Corporations of Liverpool, Birkenhead and Wallasley to promote Bills for that purpose. Following a period of vigorous lobbying and the hiring, by both sides, of eminent experts to support opposite interpretations, the parties sought accommodation, recognizing a shared interest in the port's prosperity and the avoidance of costly disputes. In 1932 they jointly proposed to the D.S.I.R. that a scientific inquiry into the issues that divided them, principally the impact of crude sewage on the amount and the hardness of deposits in the estuary, should be undertaken. After several years the conclusion was published that there was little evidence that sewage discharges affected the composition of estuary mud.[61] The M.D.H.B.'s description of the inquiry as 'eminently successful',[62] may appear surprising were it not that all parties were bound to abide with its findings without dissent as a precondition for the investigation being carried out.[63]

On Tyneside fisheries bodies had for long made representations about the river's declining condition, but to little avail. Health anxieties were more prominent than on Merseyside: gases bubbling from rotten wastes and a smell from the many outfalls so bad that it induced vomiting. Improving the Tyne's condition would, officials believed, provide benefit to inshore fishermen, reduce dredging costs, facilitate navigation, and 'get rid of conditions which must always be obnoxious, depressing and demoralizing, and ... in the heat of the summer, actually a public nuisance'.[64] Various Tyneside drainage schemes were proposed under the aegis of the Special Areas Commission. A series of reports might confirm the Tyne's nauseating condition, but crucially a risk to health could not be proved and ministerial intervention was, therefore, considered unwarranted. The local authorities were not prepared to contemplate bearing the cost of between £2.5 million and £3.5 million for such schemes, and no progress was made in developing them before 1939.

The role of the state should not be ignored. After 1945 the industrial development of estuaries was officially promoted. Central and local government supported ICI's ambitious postwar plans to expand plant on Teeside, for example, the estuary providing abundant supplies of cooling and process water, the means to dispose of liquid effluent and convenient access to imported raw materials.[65] Tyneside and Merseyside were beneficiaries of government policy to 'divert industrial development to them', in so far as they were designated as Special Areas in the mid-1930s and Development Areas in the 1950s.[66] The trend to 'position polluting industries along estuaries and along the coast' arose from several factors, including 'the ease with which liquid wastes could be discharged, especially during the period of industrialisation in the decades directly following World War II'.[67] These trends are reflected in the data summarised in Table 4.2.

Table 4.2 Industrial activity on British estuaries, 1950–70.

	1950	1970
Crude oil refining capacity in nine major estuaries ('000 tons)	9,500	109,000
Electrical generating capacity in estuarine and coastal sites (megawatts)	3,700	17,900
Steel production at BSC works discharging effluent into tidal waters ('000 tons)	5,064	10,722
Chemical industry fixed capital investment on eight estuaries (£ million, 1970 values)	204	994

Source: Royal Commission on Environmental Pollution, *Third Report: Pollution in some British estuaries and coastal waters* (London: HMSO, 1972), pp. 19–24.

This industrial development was encouraged by government in that tidal waters were deliberately excluded from the tougher pollution controls being provided for in legislative reforms enacted between 1948 and 1963. In principle, government ministers could now authorize River Boards to curtail estuarine pollution. But, in practice there was no intention to so empower the River Boards. Officials believed, as in the case of the Solent, that as estuaries were receiving 'such immense quantities of sewage and trade wastes', the costs to industry and local government of introducing new controls would be 'crippling' and out of proportion to any benefits.[68]

Superficially impartial, government departments were ready to sponsor research or conferences aimed at resolving disputes among conflicting parties. However, the state's impartiality, especially where it showed itself so in harmony with a theme dear to the heart of local government that pollution abatement schemes should be cost-effective, was not necessarily of a kind that accelerated a resolution of the underlying problems. As an official chairing a conference to consider the Tyne's pollution in 1953 stated, his department was 'not going to ask them to set about the preparation of a joint drainage scheme'.[69] As the state refused to force the issue or fund improvements estuarine pollution simply got worse.

This deterioration was tolerated for a while partly because the effects of contemporary practice were not fully appreciated. The Department of the Environment (DoE) admitted 'a dearth of information on what happens when pollutants are discharged into the marine environment', particularly regarding their absorption by, and release from, sediments.[70] However, it was gradually realised that the capacity of estuaries to scavenge the growing quantities of waste being poured into them had been 'much over-estimated'.[71] Synthesized insecticides like DDT were developed and used extensively after 1945. However, it was only in the 1960s that the apparent attraction of their stability was perceived as an environmental threat, due to the facility with which the substances entered the water cycle and accumulated in animal tissue. PCBs have similar qualities, but their presence in biological tissues was not recognized until 1966.[72] At a time when Manchester's sludge ships were discharging small amounts of PCBs, phosphorous, mercury and lead into the Irish Sea, a DoE study went out of its way to reassure that sludge dumped in coastal waters was rapidly dispersed, diluted and rendered harmless.[73] Later scientific work enumerated the consequences of these actions – high loadings of toxic chemicals, local accumulations of 'hard' substances like PCBs and phenols, and severe danger to marine life.[74]

The displacement effects of chosen policies became clearer. National surveys revealed a deterioration in tidal water quality between 1958 and 1970, which reflected, 'a shift of effluent discharge from inland to tidal waters rather than a solution to the problem as a whole'.[75] Heavily industrialised estuaries with high levels of sediment contamination became the source of further pollution in adjacent marine waters, the coasts off Merseyside and Tyneside being among those identified as pollution hot spots of heavy metal contamination, plumes of metal-contaminated estuarine waters affecting many square miles of offshore sediments.[76] North Sea coastal areas, important for the juvenile development of many commercially important fish species, were especially at risk.[77]

Modern sediment core analysis enables the historic deposition of trace metals in the Mersey estuary to be analysed and a metallic emission record to be developed for as far back as 1860 (see Figure 4.1). A steep increase in the discharge of all metals studied is shown from the third quarter of the nineteenth century, followed in most cases by emission reductions associated with industrial changes. Equally striking is that this analysis is based on the ability of estuary sediment to retain depositions of toxic metals, like arsenic, mercury and copper over extended periods of time. While reducing sewage pollution was, in principle, an uncomplicated (if vast) task, the problems caused by run-offs, often contaminated by lead, copper and cadmium, from derelict and despoiled land, including that formerly used by chemical plant or still being used for waste-disposal, presented more intractable difficulties.[78]

4.4 Estuarine rescue

In the four-stage scheme proposed in section 2 it was suggested that only in the final stage did society take decisive steps to halt the environmental decline created by the ever-growing discharge of waste into the environment, and 'invest' both through tougher regulations as well as specific programmes in a restoration of natural ecologies. The readiness to take such costly steps was attributed partly to the accumulative build-up of pollutants so that some environments close to where many people lived had become truly unpleasant. Meanwhile, changed environmental sensibilities, sharpened by the upsurge of the green movements of the 1970s, encouraged people to place a higher valuation upon environmental cleanliness. Other factors contributed to the high ranking which society placed at the end of the twentieth century on the rescue of estuarine and other tidal waters. These will now be examined in more detail, starting with general considerations before proceeding to the experience of the two estuaries during the postwar years.

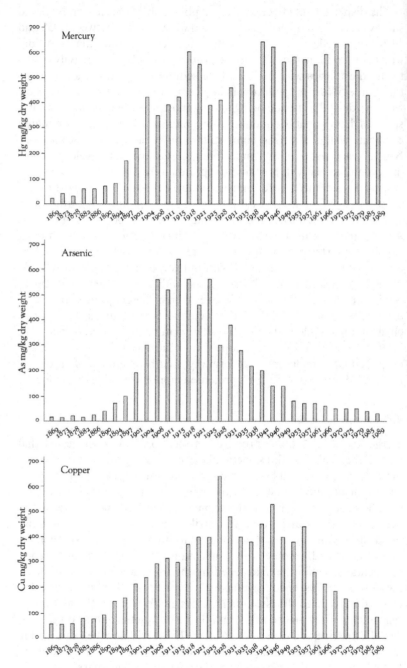

Figure 4.1 Historic metal deposition record, Widnes, River Mersey 1869–1989.

Some locally important steps were taken to improve the quality of effluent discharged into industrial rivers in the 1930s. However, the 1940s were a decade of neglect, and by the 1950s there were many symptoms of extreme crisis in the British water environment. As yet the central authorities were steadfast in their determination to resist any resolution of this crisis that would involve a substantial increase in public expenditure. By the 1950s the 'diabolical scourge' of pollution had turned rivers into 'stinking sinks and cess pools', according to an enraged anglers' association.[79] Whitehall officials privately admitted that conditions had approached a threshold of intolerability. It was acknowledged that[80]:

> ... serious pollution of the rivers may be likened to a cancerous growth which by the time it becomes evident could not be treated because of lack of resources and diversion of attention to other matters, and which has now become about as bad as it can be allowed to reach.

However, despite the growing concern for the time being little was done. A great river like the Trent had degenerated into a lifeless drain. Tidal waters were threatened by an equivalent fate. According to press reports 'England is fast becoming a jewel set in a sea, not of silver, but of sewage'.[81] The question was posed: 'Britannia may rule fewer waves than she did in the past, but has she sunk so low that she is content merely to rule a sewer?'[82]

An attitude which prevailed in the 1950s was certainly the country did face an appalling environmental problem, but at the moment it could not afford to finance its redress. The view in municipal chambers was: yes, something needs to be done, but not yet! The project to build two great interceptor sewers along both banks of the Tyne, connecting to a treatment works and sea outfall fell, a council report stated, 'into that class of work which, while desirable, need not be undertaken immediately'.[83] According to a later report, compared to the improvement of other services the restoration of the estuary was a postponable 'luxury', which might eventually be undertaken 'when other necessary improvements in the standard of living of the people of Tyneside have been completed'.[84]

On Merseyside, however, disquiet over the estuary's condition tended to turn to disgust during the 1960s: public health worries (some typhoid cases had been linked to water pollution), representations from Irish Sea fisheries, and recreational and amenity concerns were all beginning to be expressed more strongly. The reports of an energetic, if frustrated, local River Board (River Authority from 1963), and warnings, complaints and surveys from diverse sources including the Liverpool Junior Chamber of Commerce and a local Friends of the Earth group, all played their part in bringing the issue to wider notice. The Liverpool press periodically re-discovered grounds for 'shock' exposures about Britain's most polluted estuary.

A climate more conducive to intervention was beginning to emerge. Anxieties nurtured in the 1970s by global resource shocks and famines were transmitted onto more regional and local issues. Many political parties and even public opinion were being 'greened'.

The British government recognized the need for more information. 'The first step towards effective control of the pollution of coastal waters', stated the DoE, 'is to collect the facts about the existing situation'.[85] Also important was the reform of the water industry, which led to the creation of Regional Water Authorities (RWAs) in 1973 with source-to-mouth responsibility for managing the entire water cycle. Their unprecedented size, their organisational and managerial resources, their links with local government and their regional perspective, all meant that the RWAs were well-placed to perform a lead role in coordinating campaigns to rescue the estuaries and to attempt to fulfil new obligations under European Community directives. The scale of the tasks was openly admitted in that part of the RWAs' remit was to achieve, 'a massive clean-up of the country's rivers and estuaries by the early 1980s'.[86]

A significant adjustment to the policy paradigm, within which cost-effective solutions had been highly favoured, was implied by the manner in which grounds for intervention began to be presented. A report undertaken for the Royal Commission on Environmental Pollution (RCEP) stated that estuarine rehabilitation might not yield significant economic benefits, but stressed that now 'Much of the justification of pollution abatement lies in the social rather than the economic values of an aesthetically pleasant environment and of a body of water with a rich and self-sustaining ecosystem'.[87] Similarly the RCEP itself emphasized the growing recreational importance of estuaries and coastal waters and public demands for improvement in water quality 'beyond the point at which the immediate causes of chemical and biological harm are abated'. The benefits of such costly improvements were largely 'intangible', but it was necessary for pollution control, maintained the Royal Commission, to strike a balance between commercial and environmental objectives 'that is appreciated and, so far as possible, approved by the public'.[88]

Expert advisers now recognised that public demands for environmental improvement deserved to be accommodated and on more than narrow cost-benefit grounds. In the past 'consumers' of environmental goods were so diffuse that it had proved difficult for them to become an effective lobby. But with the greater significance attached to the leisure, recreational, amenity and wildlife values of coastal waters from the 1970s calls for their protection increasingly demanded the attention of politicians. If the traditional seaside resort was undergoing decline in the closing decades of the twentieth century, the advent of footloose holiday-making patterns, the growing popularity of short breaks and second holidays, the boom in water sports and the interest in eco-tourism all led to the environmental quality of coastal areas assuming greater importance. This was reflected in many developments, such as the establishment of coastal national parks after the second world war, the launch of Enterprise Neptune in 1965 and the Heritage Coast programme in 1972. Areas like the Gower peninsula and the Solent, the latter once regarded by Whitehall officials as a cheap sink for the disposal of great quantities of waste, were now viewed as important ecological assets and attractive landscape areas that offered boundless opportunities for a wide range of water and land sports within easy travelling distance of vast urban populations.

It is significant that on Merseyside the estuary's pollution first really began to animate politicians and the press locally when they began to be addressed in the context of recreational and amenity issues. The Mersey estuary system did, indeed, include waters that were used recreationally, such as Blundell Sands, even extending to Formby Point. A relevant factor in the increasing awareness of, and public impatience with, estuarine pollution, was not just the noisome smell and disgusting visual manifestations of pollution which the inhabitants had lived with for decades, but the way in which the bathing water controversy resonated locally. A Royal Society of Health Conference held in Liverpool Town Hall thoroughly explored the issue in the same year, 1963, that the President of Coastal Anti-Pollution League, Tony Wakefield, was invited to address a meeting of Merseyside local authorities on the subject.[89] The worsening pollution over the following years was reported increasingly in terms of the health and amenity hazards it created.[90] It was felt that even Southport's beaches came into 'the firing line' from the raw effluent discharged from the estuary's 187 sewage outfalls and 136 industrial plants. The impact which environmental decline could have on a tourist economy was graphically demonstrated by the fate of Merseyside's own seaside resort, New Brighton. A variety of influences led to the town being almost destroyed as a coastal amusement centre in the 1960s, but environmental factors including beach erosion and the filthy stench and visual conditions at the mouth of the estuary helped to make the situation virtually irretrievable.[91] Notwithstanding the exceptional counter-trend achievements of Blackpool, coastal pollution played a major role in damaging the reputation of Lancashire's entire holiday coast, particularly for Morecambe.

Rising incomes and growing environmental awareness, changing leisure patterns, and new commitments under European Community environmental law, all conspired to change the politics of coastal pollution. This was an issue vigorously taken up not only by groups such as Greenpeace, but also by the consumer movement and the media. The Which magazine devoted considerable attention to it, for example in the issues of July 1973 and July 1975, and many reviews and newspapers have frequently revisited it.[92] Also imparting a consumers rights flavour to the agitation for a massive improvement in coastal water quality, the two organisations most actively, often militantly, leading it, the Marine Conservation Society and Surfers Against Sewage, while seeking to champion broader causes, arose out of the concerns of two quite narrow recreational groups, divers and surfers.

These developments partly explain why the projects to revive the estuaries of the Mersey and Tyne have generated such enormous enthusiasm and interest from public, private, educational and voluntary bodies. To these we finally turn.

A collective sewage disposal scheme for Tyneside had originally been proposed in 1931. Government-sponsored conferences gathered local government and other interested parties together in the 1950s, from which emerged initiatives that led to the establishment of the Tyneside Sewerage Board in 1966. The Northumbrian Water Authority pressed ahead with this project in 1974. Merseyside local authorities had first engaged in serious talks about the estuary's pollution in 1963.[93] Later protests and pressures led the River Authority to call for action in 1971, which led local authorities, industrialists and water interests to set up a Steering Group to further investigate the problem. From 1974 the North West Water Authority sought to develop more concrete proposals but it was hamstrung by financial cut-backs. Eventually, Michael Heseltine having declared that the state of the Mersey was 'an affront to the standards a civilized society should demand of its citizens',[94] government interest was secured, and the £3 billion Mersey Basin Campaign was launched by the Department of the Environment in 1985.

Modest signs of improvement in water quality in the Mersey estuary could be detected in the late 1960s. Over the following years effluent was improved so that its ammonia content fell, the overall pollution load as registered by BOD began to decline and rising levels of dissolved oxygen were recorded (see Figure 4.2 and plates). With the completion of modern STWs, the organic constituents of sewage waste were considerably reduced and the estuary's assimilative capacity was progressively restored. By the 1990s water quality in both estuaries had been significantly raised according to a range of indicators, most dramatically expressed in the return of many long-absent species including squid, octopus and sea trout to the Mersey.

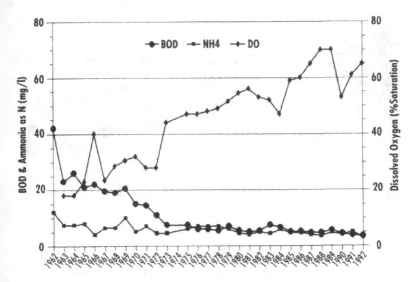

Figure 4.2 Water quality indicators at Howley Weir, River Mersey (mean annual values).

Plate 1: The Mersey restored.

Plate 2: A recent view of the Mersey estuary.

   In conclusion, the two estuarine case studies have illustrated many of the difficulties which have complicated the tasks of not just coastal environmental management but of pollution control generally since the industrial revolution: how economic expansion leads not only to the increased exploitation of natural resources, but also the parallel growth in the volume of waste matter, critical loads being exceeded, and an increase in pollution; how policy difficulties such as the multiple-use and public good characteristics of common resources compromised attempts to develop acceptable and effective strategies to deal with such problems, leading to their spatial and temporal displacement; finally, when the social costs caused by neglect proved unacceptable, rescue programmes were put in place. Despite their great cost these campaigns have generated a huge amount of regional support. This has been explained not solely because a more affluent society finds environmental protection more affordable. The rescue of estuarine waters, complementing programmes of urban renewal, was consonant with society's readiness to assess the worth of such projects in more than narrow monetary terms, but with reference also to recreational, amenity and other values. It was no longer tenable to view the filthy environment of a polluted estuary as the unavoidable consequence of economic progress.

Notes

* I should like to express gratitude to Roger Fouquet and Bruce Philp for providing extensive comments on this paper. All errors are the author's responsibility. Thanks are due to the Environment Agency for giving permission to use material employed in figures one and two, the former being based on work carried out by the Industrial Ecology Centre at Liverpool University. I would also like to express thanks to the Mersey Basin Campaign for providing the photographs of the estuary and the map of the Mersey catchment.

1 J. F. Richards, 'World environmental history and economic development', in W. C. Clark and R. E. Munns (eds), *Sustainable development of the biosphere* (Cambridge: Cambridge University Press, 1986), p. 54; D. Worster, 'Doing environmental history', in D. Worster (ed.), *The ends of the earth: perspectives on modern environmental history* (Cambridge: Cambridge University Press, 1988), pp. 289–90; I. Massa, 'The paradox of insignificant change: perspectives on environmental history', *Environmental History Newsletter*, V (1993), p. 12; M. Chase, 'Can history be green? A prognosis', *Environmental History Newsletter*, IV (1992), pp. 3–9; 11; A. W. Crosby, 'The past and present of environmental history', *American Historical Review*, C (1995), p. 1181.

2 E. L. Jones, 'The environment and the economy', in P. Burke (ed.), *The New Cambridge Modern History*, vol. XIII, *Companion Volume* (Cambridge: Cambridge University Press, 1979), p. 15.

3 A. M. Mannion, *Global environmental change: a natural and cultural environmental history* (Harlow: Longman, 1991), p. 141; C. Pfister, and P. Brimblecombe, 'Introduction', in P. Brimblecombe and C. Pfister (eds), *The silent countdown: essays in European environmental history* (Berlin: Springer-Verlag, 1990), p. 5.

4 C. Hamlin, *What becomes of pollution? Adversary science and controversy on the self-purification of rivers in Britain, 1850–1900* (New York: Garland Publishing, 1987); J. Sheail, 'Town wastes, agricultural sustainability and Victorian sewage', *Urban History*, XXIII (1996), pp. 189–210. B. Luckin, *Pollution and control: a social history of the Thames in the nineteenth century* (Bristol: Adam Hilger, 1986).

5 A. E. Dingle, '"The monster nuisance of All": landowners, alkali manufacturers and air pollution, 1828–1864', *Economic History Review*, 2nd ser., XXXV (1982), pp. 529–48.

6 G. Hardin, 'The tragedy of the commons', *Science*, CLXXII (1968), pp. 1243–8.

7 R. van Ginkel, 'The abundant sea and her fates: Texelian oystermen and the marine commons', *Comparative Studies in Society and History*, XXXVIII (1996), pp. 218–42.

8 M. Douglas, *Implicit meanings: essays in anthropology* (London: Routledge, 1975).

9 M. Douglas and A. Wildavsky, *Risk and culture: an essay on the selection of technological and environmental dangers* (Berkeley: University of California Press, 1983).

10 D. Pearce, 'The limits to cost-benefit analysis as a guide to environmental policy', *Kyklos*, XXIX (1976), pp. 97–112.

11 C. L. Spash and R. C. d'Arge, 'The greenhouse effect and intergenerational transfers', *Energy Policy*, XVII (1989), pp. 88–96.
12 K. Smith, *Water in Britain: a study in applied hydrology* (London: Macmillan, 1972), pp. 172–3.
13 Jones, *The environment*, p. 27.
14 S. W. Humphrey, and J. Stansilaw (1979) 'Economic growth and energy consumption in the UK, 1700–1975', *Energy Policy*, VII (1979), pp. 29–42.
15 J. Hassan, *A history of water in modern England and Wales* (Manchester: Manchester University Press, 1998).
16 R. Fouquet and P. J. G. Pearson, 'A thousand years of energy use in the United Kingdom', *The Energy Journal*, XIX (1998), p. 26.
17 Hassan, *Water in England*, p. 15.
18 A. S. Wohl, *Endangered lives: public health in Victorian Britain* (London: Methuen, 1983), p. 208.
19 P. Brimblecombe, *The big smoke: a history of air pollution in London since medieval times* (London: Routledge, 1987), p. 117; J. H. Niven and C. H. Tattersall, 'Meteorology and the health of Manchester and Salford', in British Medical Association, *Handbook and guide to Manchester* (Manchester: F. Ireland, 1902), p. 40.
20 B. Gustaffson, 'Nature and economy', in M. Teich, R. Porter and B. Gustafsson (eds), *Nature and society in historical context* (Cambridge: Cambridge University Press, 1997), pp. 347–363.
21 P. J. G. Pearson, 'Energy, externalities and environmental quality: will development cure the ills it creates?' *Energy Studies Review*, VI (1994), pp. 201–2.
22 Pearce, 'limits to cost-benefit analysis'.
23 H. Jones, 'The sea and the sea-side', *The Cornhill Magazine*, LXII (August, 1890), p. 191.
24 Wohl, *Endangered lives*, p. 256.
25 Public Record Office (hereafter PRO), M 16/1, H. Philips to R. Angus Smith, 17 Feb. 1881.
26 Pearson, 'Energy and environmental quality'.
27 PRO, HLG 50/2052, Newcastle-upon-Tyne, 'Main Drainage Report', 1949.
28 A. Biggs, 'A geographical study of water resources of England and Wales and their use in large scale supplies of piped water to cities' (unpublished Ph.D. thesis, University of London, 1949).
29 Liverpool, City of, *Handbook compiled for the Congress of the Royal Institute of Public Health* (Liverpool: the Corporation, 1903), p. 220.
30 (Jeger Report), Ministry of Housing and Local Government, Welsh Office, *Taken for Granted: Report of the working party on sewage disposal* (London: HMSO, 1970), pp. 1–3.
31 Liverpool Record Office (hereafter LRO), City of Liverpool Council Proceedings, *Annual Report of the Medical Officer of Health*, 1927.
32 F. G. Hardy, S. M. Evans, M. A. Tremayne, 'Long-term changes in the marine macroalgae of three polluted estuaries in north-east England', *Journal of experimental marine biology and ecology*, CLXXII (1993), p. 81.
33 A. Netbuoy, *The Atlantic Salmon* (London: Faber, 1968), pp. 175, 210.
34 PRO, HLG 50/25, L. Warner to Mersey Harbour Board, 28 Jan. 1927.
35 E. Porter, *Pollution in four industrialised estuaries* (London: HMSO, 1973), p. 19.
36 Porter, *four estuaries*, p. 43.

37 Netbuoy, *Atlantic salmon*, p. 207.
38 Manchester Central Library (hereafter MCL), A. Meek, *The pollution of the River Tyne*, 15 March 1927.
39 PRO, HLG 50/2051, 'Report of the Tyne Sewage Committee', 31 Jan. 1936.
40 Tyneside Joint Sewerage Board, *Tyneside Joint Sewerage Board 1966–1974: the polluted Tyne* (Newcastle: Sewerage Board, 1974).
41 Porter, *four estuaries*, pp. 42–3.
42 National Rivers Authority, *The Mersey estuary: a report on environmental quality* (Bristol: NRA, 1995) p. 28.
43 E. Porter, *Water management in England and Wales* (Cambridge: Cambridge University Press, 1978), p. 120.
44 Hamlin, *Adversary science*, pp. 547–53.
45 C. Hamlin, 'Muddling in Bumbledon: on the enormity of large sanitary improvements in four British towns', 1855–1885, *Victorian Studies*, XXXII (1988), pp. 55–83; J. Sheail, 'Sewering the English suburbs: an inter-war perspective', *Journal of Historical Geography*, XIX (1993), pp. 445–6.
46 G. D. Elsdon, 'Sanitation and water purification', *Reports of the Progress of Applied Chemistry*, XXVI (1941), pp. 470–87.
47 Hassan, *Water in England*, p. 29; F. Bell, and R. Millward, 'Public health expenditure and mortality in Britain 1870–1914', *Continuity and Change* (1998).
48 J. G. Lloyd. and J. B. Oldfield, 'Planning for cleaning up an estuary Part I: concepts and organisation', *Journal of the Institution of water engineers and scientists*, XXXI (1977), p. 319.
49 D. Tromp, 'Coastal pollution in northern Europe', in Institute of Civil Engineers, *Proceedings of the Conference on coastal discharges: engineering aspects and experience* (London: Thomas Telford, 1981), p. 14.
50 Bury Reference Library, County Borough of Bury, 'Report for the case for the corporation in the action brought by the Mersey and Irwell Joint Committee', 1900; *Macclesfield Courier*, 12 Sept. 1892.
51 MCL, House of Commons, *Mersey and Irwell (Prevention of Pollution) Bill*, petitions against the Bill, 1892; MCL, R. A. Tatton, *Report to the Mersey and Irwell Joint Committee*, April 1902.
52 Sheail, 'Town wastes', p. 209.
53 C. Hamlin, 'William Dibdin and the idea of biological sewage treatment', *Technology and Culture*, XXIX (1985), pp. 196–7.
54 J. Sheail, 'An historical perspective on the development of a marine resource: the Whitstable oyster fishery', *Marine Environmental Research*, XIX (1986), p. 285.
55 Hassan, *Water in England*, p. 34.
56 Wohl, *Endangered lives*, pp. 254–5.
57 J. Hassan, 'Dealing with coastal pollution in health resorts in England and Wales, 1800–1960: policies and politics of local authorities', *Yearbook of European Administrative History*, XI (1999), p. 170.
58 PRO, HLG 50/25, City of Liverpool, Report re discharge of crude sewage into the River Mersey, 1930.
59 LRO, City of Liverpool, *Annual report of the Medical Officer of Health*, 1927, p. 232.
60 MCL, Acting Conservator of the Mersey, *Annual report on the state of the navigation of the Mersey*, 1930, pp. 13–14.

61 D.S.I.R., *The effect of the discharge of raw sewage into the estuary of the River Mersey*, WPRT Paper 7 (London: HMSO, 1938).

62 MCL, Acting Conservator of the Mersey, *Annual report on the state the navigation of the Mersey*, 1939, p. 13.

63 PRO, HLG 50/23, joint letter from M.D.H.B. and Liverpool town clerk to D.S.I.R., 7 Oct. 1932.

64 PRO, HLG 50/2051, C. Addison to A. Greenwood, 16 Feb. 1931.

65 PRO, HLG 71/685, 'The Wilton Works project', 9 Oct. 1945.

66 W. Luttrell, *Factory location and industrial movement: a study of recent experience in Great Britain*, vol. I (London: NIESR, 1962), p. 68.

67 Tromp, 'Coastal pollution', p. 6.

68 PRO, HLG 50/2075, report on Rivers Act 1951, 12 Jan. 1955.

69 PRO, HLG 50/2052, report of meeting of Tyneside local authorities, 3 Feb. 1953.

70 Department of the Environment, Central Unit on Environmental Pollution, *Monitoring the marine environment of the United Kingdom. First report of the marine pollution monitoring management group 1975–76* (London: HMSO, 1977), p. 16.

71 B. A. Southgate, *Water: pollution and conservation* (Harrow: Thunderbird, 1969), p. 124.

72 Tromp, 'Coastal pollution', p. 7.

73 Department of the Environment, *Out of Sight, Out of Mind: report of the working party on sludge disposal in Liverpool Bay*, vol. III (London: HMSO, 1973).

74 P. A. Johnston, R. L. Stringer, and M. C. French, 'Pollution of UK estuaries: historical and current problems', *The Science of the Total Environment*, CVI (1991), pp. 55–70.

75 D. J. Parker and E. C. Penning-Rowsell, *Water Planning in Britain* (London: G. Allen & Unwin, 1980), p. 112.

76 Tromp, 'Coastal pollution'; J. A. Hall, C. J. J. Frid, and R. K. Proudfoot, 'Effects of metal contamination on the macrobenthos of two North Sea estuaries', *Journal of Marine Science*, LIII (1996), pp. 1014–23.

77 P. C. Wood, 'The discharge of sewage from sea outfalls into the North Sea', in A. L. H. Game-son (ed.), *Discharge of Sewage from sea outfalls* (Oxford: Pergamon, 1975), p. 6.

78 J. Handley, 'The land of Merseyside', in W. T. S. Gould and A. G. Hodgkiss eds., *The resources of Merseyside* (Liverpool: Liverpool University Press, 1982), pp. 83–100.

79 PRO, HLG 50/2850, Coventry and District Anglers Association, telegram, 5 June 1957.

80 PRO, HLG 50/2850, Notes on river pollution, Nov. 1957.

81 'Britain is investigating polio theory', *New York Times*, 18 Aug. 1957.

82 Editorial, *The Medical Press*, 26 Aug. 1959, pp. 163–4.

83 PRO, HLG 50/2052, Newcastle-upon-Tyne, 'Main drainage report', 1949.

84 Newcastle upon Tyne, City and Council of, *Report to be presented for consideration at the Council Meeting* (Newcastle Town Improvement and Street Committee, 28 July 1958), p. 11.

85 Department of the Environment, Welsh Office, *Report of a survey of the discharge of foul sewage to the coastal waters England and Wales* (London: HMSO, 1973), p. v.

86 Department of the Environment, *foul sewage*, p. 8.
87 Porter, *four estuaries*, p. 94.
88 Royal Commission on Environmental Pollution, *Tenth report: Tackling pollution – experience and prospects* (London: HMSO, 1984), p. 66.
89 *Liverpool Daily Post,* 12 Nov. 1963.
90 *Liverpool Daily Post*, 6 Oct. 1970; *Liverpool Echo*, 27 Oct. 1970.
91 J. Demetriadi, 'The golden years: English seaside resorts 1950–1974', in G. Shaw and A. Williams eds., *The rise and fall of the British seaside resorts: cultural and economic perspectives* (London: Pinter, 1997), p. 73.
92 'Bathing, sewage and illness', *Which*, July 1973, pp. 196–9; 'Seaside sewage revisited', *Which*, July 1975, pp. 206–8.
93 *Liverpool Daily Post*, 12 Nov. 1963.
94 North West Water Authority, *Annual report and accounts for 1982/83* (Warrington: NWWA, 1983), p. 14.

Index

Note: **Bold** page numbers refer to tables; *Italic* page numbers refer to figures and page numbers followed by "n" denote endnotes.

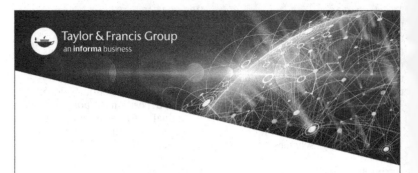

Taylor & Francis Group
an **informa** business

Taylor & Francis eBooks

www.taylorfrancis.com

A single destination for eBooks from Taylor & Francis
with increased functionality and an improved user
experience to meet the needs of our customers.

90,000+ eBooks of award-winning academic content in
Humanities, Social Science, Science, Technology, Engineering,
and Medical written by a global network of editors and authors.

TAYLOR & FRANCIS EBOOKS OFFERS:

A streamlined
experience for
our library
customers

A single point
of discovery
for all of our
eBook content

Improved
search and
discovery of
content at both
book and
chapter level

REQUEST A FREE TRIAL
support@taylorfrancis.com

Printed in the United States
by Baker & Taylor Publisher Services

Printed in the United States
by Baker & Taylor Publisher Services